Seeing
is
Believing

Set in Times Roman type and printed
in Ireland by O'Brien Promotions Limited,
Barrow Street, Dublin
for the publishers
PILGRIM PRESS
The Lodge, Mountrath, Co. Laois, Ireland

First published 1985
ISBN 0 85105 371 8

Seeing is Believing

MOVING STATUES IN IRELAND

Edited by

COLM TÓIBÍN

Maryanne Felter
July 2011.

PILGRIM PRESS

CONTRIBUTORS

Eanna Brophy is a staff journalist with *The Sunday Press*.

Tommie Gorman is North Western correspondent for RTE.

Isabel Healy is a journalist and broadcaster living in Cork.

Mary Holland is a journalist and broadcaster who writes regularly for *The Observer* and *The Irish Times*.

Peter Kellner is Political Editor of *The New Statesman*.

June Levine is a journalist and author of "Sisters", a memoir of the Irish feminist movement.

Nell McCafferty's books include "In the Eyes of the Law" and 'The Best of Nell".

Eamonn McCann is a journalist and broadcaster who writes regularly for *The Sunday World* and *In Dublin*. He is the author of "War in an Irish Town".

Kevin D. O'Connor is a journalist and broadcaster. His books include "The Irish in Britain".

Breandán Ó hEithir is the author of "Lig Sinn in gCathu' and "Over the Bar: A Personal Relationship with the GAA".

Dáithí Ó hÓgáin lectures in Folklore at UCD. His books include "An File", a study of the image of the poet in the Irish tradition and "The Hero in Irish Folk History".

Fintan O'Toole is Editor of *Magill* magazine.

Francis Stuart is Ireland's leading novelist. His books include "Blacklist Section H", "Pillar of Cloud" and "The High Consistory".

Colm Tóibín is a freelance journalist living in Dublin.

Contents

I

A crowd at Ballinspittle   *(photo Billy MacGill)*

Introduction

Check this

There is a poem by George Herbert entitled "Prayer" which lists some of the properties and qualities of prayer with simply a comma between each item on the list. There is a sense in the poem that the list is not exhaustive nor definitive. It is as though the items were merely instalments in a series without end which could be added to and taken away from without much trouble. Prayer, in Herbert's view, is a bottomless well. Some of his epitets for prayer seem obvious and clear ("The soul in paraphrase, heart in pilgrimage"); others are striking and somewhat difficult to make out ("Exalted Manna, gladnesse of the best"). The reader can pick and choose among the items, reject some, ponder on others, accept the rest, and even perhaps add some more.

So it is with the reasons why, in the spring and summer of 1985 in the Republic of Ireland, thousands of people have been going to Marian shrines, some later claiming that they saw statues move, or visions, or lights in the sky. The reasons would be on the lines of Herbert's poem: a random list containing the obvious and the obscure which the reader could feel a right to accept or reject or add to.

The Kerry Babies Tribunal, the bad weather, the Air India crash, the death of Ann Lovett, the national debt, facts and divisions which came to light during the Amendment debate, unemployment, the hunger strikes in the North, boring television programmes in the summer, the failure of Garret FitzGerald to improve the lot of anyone in the country, simple piety, nostalgia for the happiness and harmony induced by the Papal visit, fear that the church has moved too far away from things of the spirit and too far into the public domain, simple curiosity, the feeling that more sin is being committed than ever before, the sense that things cannot go on as they have been going, the need to pray in the darkness in the company of others.

The list may apply to some and not to others. At the end of Herbert's poem "Prayer", however, there is a resolution. Instead of the commas which divide the items on the list, there is a semi-colon followed by two words: "something understood", simply that. The poem ends. It is, unfortunately, impossible to resolve our list in this way, except by adding the word "not". Something not understood. Why not?

Rural Ireland remains a mystery, even to itself. Things which we presume to be true about life, belief and habit in the south and west of the country are probably false. There is a general view that from the 1960's onwards things changed beyond belief: bungalows were built, methods of farming were altered, education was free, roads were improved, grants from the EEC replaced the American mail, discos were held, lounge bars were opened, emigration ceased. And there is a general view too that attitudes changed accordingly, helped along by television, radio and shifting standards among the newspapers. Things would never be the same again.

The contrary, however, may be closer to the truth. Those who benefited from economic change may have become more conservative, all the better to hold that which they have. The future may be full of promise but the past is where certainty lay, where harmony existed, where people knew what to believe in.

Conor Cruise O'Brien in a radio interview on his visit to Ballinspittle expressed surprise at the number of middle class people he saw there. It is likely that commentators and journalists will continue to express surprise and wonder at the happenings and attitudes in rural Ireland in the future. They may not conform to what we expected to happen or what we think happened. Only a handful of journalists and a handful of writers manage to offer a sense of what is really going on outside the cities.

This book is a bit like George Herbert's poem too, although some of it is rather more profane. There is no attempt to be definitive nor exhaustive. Half the pieces are published exactly as they appeared in print with the date and name of publication at the bottom. The other seven were commissioned especially for this book. (The exception is Isabel Healy's article — the first half was commissioned and the second half was first printed in *IT* magazine).

Many other facets of this issue need to be written about. The attitude of the church, for example, to the moving statues, and the public pronouncements of the bishops will require careful study. The whole question of optical illusion also needs to be dealt with. This collection of essays and articles is merely a first step.

Part I of this book consists of reports from the shrine at Ballinspittle. Part II analyses the significance and cultural context of the moving statues phenomenon. Part III looks at moving statues in other parts of the country.

Colm Tóibín,
September 1985.

The statue at Ballinspittle   *(photo Billy MacGill)*

I

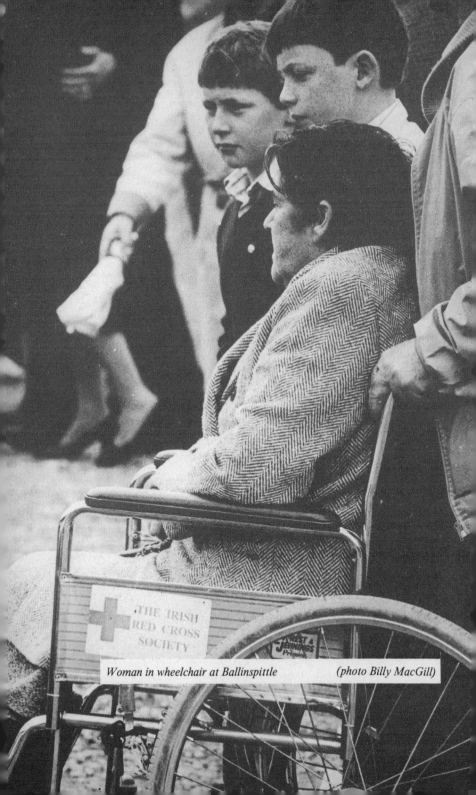

THE IRISH
RED CROSS
SOCIETY

Woman in wheelchair at Ballinspittle   (photo Billy MacGill)

What I Saw In Ballinspittle

June Levine

It all started on a drenching day about three weeks ago. The taxi driver told me he was going to Lourdes on his holidays. He looked like a man who'd be more at ease staring into the froth of a freshly poured pint. "Why are you going?" I asked him.

"To pray for all sinnners," he said simply, obviously including himself.

"There's a lot of us about," I said and we talked of other things. As I left the car, he called after me: "I won't forget to say one for you. I'll remember . . ."

I should have asked him if he'd fancy a run to Ballinspittle, I thought, and recall being surprised that such an idea had been somewhere in my head. The seed sprouted and I decided I'd write a piece about why people might *think* they were seeing concrete statues move.

My favourite theory was that it was not the statue, but Mary, moving in the hearts of Irish Christians who are terribly depressed these times. The country was never more in need of mothering, I decided, the sort of mothering that could only come from a Mother of unquestionable Power. I would also write that deep in the psyche of this race are memories of the Great Mother Goddess Danu of pre-Celtic times after whose people The Tuaithe de Dana, the Paps (breasts) of Danu, the twin mountains in Kerry are named.

Thoughts take wings, and I soon found myself with a friend on the way to Cork en route to Ballinspittle. "If you hadn't gone, you wouldn't be in this predicament," a man told me upon my return. 'This predicament,' is that I saw the face of the statue of the Virgin Mary change. The 'moving statue' did not move, but the face changed. I saw it. It did so several times. I tried to talk myself out of it, but my friend also saw it and so did others in the crowd.

People who have not been to Ballinspittle keep explaining to me what *really* happened, while others dismiss the idea out of hand. Many people's rudeness can only be put down to religious bigotry. I have re-discovered that the latter takes many forms. For instance, it is not permissable in certain circles to see what one is not supposed to see. There is a concrete explanation for everything. People who threaten this concept must be deluded, hysterical or lying.

"If that happened to me it would change my whole life," said a nice woman who looked at my yellow dress in a way that made me feel I should be wearing sack cloth. There is no chance of it happening to her at Ballinspittle because she "wouldn't be seen dead going to Ballinspittle." Thank heaven for people with open minds.

There would not be a bus going to Ballinspittle until 8 o'clock that night so we had to get a taxi. The taxi driver told us he hadn't seen anything himself, but "I have to believe in it because my wife was cured of arthritis. They say the statue moves, forward and back and that the head moves from side to side and the hands move." He told us of other moving statues around the area.

Gerald O'Loughlin had gone to the grotto four times at night and stood in "huge crowds", but did not see anything unusual. His wife Kathleen was in great pain with her feet and legs and "it was fierce for her getting down to pray, but she got up without a bother. The pain was gone. It took a few days for the swelling to go, but the pain went like that. "She didn't see the statue move the first time, but she did on subsequent visits. Kathleen goes to mass at 7.30 every morning, and as we drove back into town that night with her husband, she came on the car radio to tell her husband that she was off to Mass.

There was a small crowd in front of the statue that Saturday afternoon at about 3 o'clock. The sun shone and it was windy. There were young families with grand-parents, teenagers in jeans, groups of women and individuals. A woman was leading the Rosary from some distance away through a loud speaker.

A few people kneeled on the bench in front of the rail around the hill. There are a few benches for seating. We stood awhile and then went and sat on the front bench. The woman was still saying the Rosary. Every time she said: ". . . blessed art thous amonst wimming," we smiled at each other, but my friend soon joined in.

I put on my glasses. My friend was wearing her contact lenses. The face of the statue was quite lovely and I forced myself not to

14

stare, that might cause my eyes to play tricks. I blinked and looked away and looked back again.

I had done this several times, I think, when I saw the face change. The chin became dark with beard and thinking it was caused by a cloud passing overhead, I thought: "that doesn't do much for her." It was not a cloud. Gradually, the face changed altogether and I recognised the kindly though strong face of a very young rabbi. I thought: "he's only a boy, his beard is not fully grown." The veil of the statue covered his dark hair and I realised that now it was not a veil, but a Jewish prayer shawl. "My" rabbi looked real and so young, perhaps in his teens. The head turned back into the image of Mary again.

I felt under tremendous pressure as though energy was pressing in on me from everyone else and my heart ached. I kept silent, not wanting to influence my friend. I don't know how long it took, but eventually she gripped my arm and said: "June, can you see the face of Our Lord? Oh God, it is changing. June, what do I see?"

"I can't tell you what you see, you tell me," I said. We sat there arguing with our own experience, but becoming more and more sure of the changes. I could feel the shape of my heart inside my chest and it was sore. I recall rubbing my left arm and at the same time being aware that my heart was never healthier.

On the other side of my friend a young woman sobbed. She was seeing the changes and she asked did we see the face of Padre Pio? My friend had not seen a rabbi, nor someone so young, but she saw something else which I did not see, a third change. She says it was somebody blonde or a head bathed in light.

There was a group of three middle-aged women behind. The Rosary through the loud-speaker had ended some time ago. Now, a spontaneous Rosary erupted. "Hail Mary full of Grace, it's an optical illusion," said one of the women behind, "blessed art thou among women, it is only imagination, I don't see anything . . ."

The praying became remarkable. I have been in places of worship all over the world. In synagogues, temples, chapels, churches, and make-shift shrines and been with people repeating the same old words, seeming to be worn smooth with use. This was different. I was amazed by the energy of this prayer. The only time I have experienced anything like it was in the presence of Shri Ram Chandra, a man of great holiness in an ashram in India.

Some distance away there was a man with binoculars. "Ask him to lend them to us?" I asked my friend. She went and brought them back and had difficulty locating the statue through them. And then she said: "Oh," with a mixture of surprise and disappointment. Silently, she handed the binoculars to me.

I looked up at the statue and was shocked. The statue was as I had never seen it before, ordinary, crude. The plastered 'face' was unreal, vacant. The features were badly shaped and the eyes were the biggest shock of all. They merely *represented* eyes, daubs of bright blue paint in the middle of each indentation (no cornea) and there was a black spot on the cheek which may have been a chip in the plaster.

"This is the optical illusion," I thought, "it can't be what has been there all the time. I've never seen it before . . ." What I had seen was a fine boned, refined, woman's face. I have since realised that when I saw the face change, so did the body beneath the robes, becoming frail, masculine though boyish.

Without the binoculars we saw the same as we had seen before. For me, a young Rabbi and Mary. For my friend: "Our Lord and His Mother and I think, the Holy Ghost." Some people were seeing changes, some were not. Most were praying. We sat a while.

Suddenly, my friend said: "We'll miss our train. Do you realise we've been here for two hours." It felt like ten minutes. But not really. There had been no sense of time. Looking back time *was* different. I liked it there and had no wish to leave.

"We'll go and see can we find Ann," said my friend. "If she is at home in Cork she'll drive us back out tonight. We'll call from the station and if she isn't there we'll go back to Dublin. I have to be back in Dublin to-night." My friend was confused. A highly disciplined person, she did not want to neglect her duty in Dublin, but did not want to leave. Without realising it, we decided that Ann would decide. As I walked away from the grotto on the hill, I knew that leaving would not be easier later or even next day. Ann was not available. We left Cork on the 6.45 p.m. train.

I've been trying to rationalise what happened. I've read piles of stuff by the "experts". I've talked to people of various temperaments and academic disciplines. And I've decided to give myself a break and stop searching for an analysis of that which cannot be analysed.

I saw the statue change. I'm delighted about that. What does it mean? For me, personally, time will tell. But thoughts keep coming. For instance, we have contempt for mere concrete, but how concrete do we try to make our living, our experience. Why? People are depressed and worried about material things, and have reason to be, especially in the Cork area.

I do not under-estimate the importanc of survival, especially in these times. However, it occurs to me that Ireland has become increasingly materialistic. Perhaps, Someone is reminding us that rich or poor, we perish altogether if we live by bread alone.

Southside, 11 September.

A Miracle At Ballinspittle

Isabel Healy

On 31 July, a thirty seven year old Cork housewife who has been completely deaf since she was twenty, claims that she had her hearing restored during a visit to the grotto at Ballinspittle.

Mrs Frances O'Riordan from the North side of Cork city got measles when she was four years of age, and over the next seventeen years her hearing gradually diminished, until at twenty, she was "stone deaf." She first visited Ballinspittle on 31 July, with her husband Donal, her sister and sister-in-law. Standing on the hillside with her sister soon after ten o'clock on that dark, dry night, Frances saw a movement in the statue, and felt strange sensations in herself. "My body felt as though it was exploding, and I thought I was going to choke — and then I heard it — the crowd singing 'Ave Maria' — those were the first words I heard 'Ave Maria.' I told my sister, and she knew I couldn't be lip-reading because it was so dark, and she just said 'take it easy, take your time — so I stayed quiet for a while, listening, and the singing stopped and the rosary began — I thought they were all roaring, because it was so strange, but my sister said it was just a normal sound."

"When we were walking back to the car I kept asking my sister 'who is banging those two tin cans beside us?' But it was no banging — my sister told me it was just her high heels on the road — but I'd never heard that sound before. I was terribly excited," and, said Mrs O'Riordan, the mother of four children aged 11 to 3 years, she told nobody. "I was afraid it would be gone again in the morning, but the next day I heard my little three year old boy crying for the very first time — and I heard the doorbell, that was a lovely tinkley 'ding-dong' — the doorbell is lovely."

Mrs O'Riordan is none too happy with the sounds so familiar to the hearing that we no longer notice, but positively frightening to one who had never heard a modern city. "The noise in town is ferocious, I went shopping a few days later, and I had to run out of Patrick Street because I was afraid to cross the road with the noise of the buses — and then when I got into the bus, there were all sounds of the ticket machine and the money tinkling into the bus conductor's bag, and I even had to turn down the television."

Mrs O'Riordan, a small woman with short grey hair, dressed in a pink dress and white jacket, and drinking orange squash when I met her in the bar of the Imperial Hotel in Cork on 16 September, seems like a decent, sensible, and jolly woman. At first she was shy, explaining that for so long she had not socialised, because it was too embarrassing to be left on the sidelines, and she couldn't lip-read in a gathering, but as she told her story she became very lively, and sometimes emotional, about the hugeness of the experience to her life. Her speech has the slight "thickness" of those who learn to speak without hearing, and she said the first time she heard her own voice, it was so loud inside her, she cried.

Wearing a new hearing aid, which had been fitted recently, she sat beside her sister-in-law and husband Donal, a quiet and easy going man, and explained that she did not want her address or photograph published as she was afraid of being recognised, and wanted to remain anonymous. When she visited the doctor recently, and had the hearing aid fitted, she was told she had "nearly 30% hearing" by her doctor, who had no wish to comment on the case "for twelve months at least."

Three years ago, Frances had gone to an eminent eye, ear, nose and throat specialist at a Cork hospital, in the hope of having an operation, but was told there was nothing the medics could do as both her ear drums were permanently and irreparably damaged. She learned to lip read, and resigned herself to a world of silence, and a reticence to talk because she could not hear herself. The family decided to go to Ballinspittle, mostly out of curiosity, but Frances, who had three times been to Knock, said she had prayed to Our Lady to help her at Ballinspittle. "I'm not a very religious person at all," she said cheerfully, "I can't get to daily Mass with the children, and this has not made me 'religious mad'. I went to the local priest — but he said to wait for twelve months before anything could be proven — but I'd go to the Pope in Rome if he wanted to see for himself — I firmly believe I was cured in Ballinspittle."

As the O'Riordans moved house recently, neither her current family doctor nor her local priest are those who knew her over the years when she was deaf.

For some time Frances and her family kept what they feel is a miracle to themselves, but after visiting Ballinspittle several times, they thought they should tell the grotto committee. "We were delighted, and we did believe Mrs O'Riordan," said a lady member of the committee that night. (Two committee members had joined us, they were up in town for a swim in the pool of the Spastic Clinic in Ballintemple). "We have been told of three other cases of healing at the grotto recently, but the details are not yet available. They concern a man cured of the results of a stroke, a woman with arthritis who had left her walking stick behind her at the grotto, and a handicapped child. We believe the stories, but we do not want to raise people's hopes too much as yet."

Frances O'Riordan still finds some difficulty in tuning in to all the sounds in a gathering, but she says "30% hearing might seem little to you, but to me it is amazing — my whole world has changed. When I got my hearing back first, I was always afraid it was a dream, and I'd wake up deaf again, but now I am convinced I've got it back for good — and it was Our Lady of Ballinspittle who did it. I don't know why *me* — but what else could it be — I went down deaf, and standing on the hillside in the dark I heard my first words 'Ave Maria'."

During the day, you don't notice the traffic so much, because Ballinspittle is about ten miles past Kinsale, and the Kinsale road is always crowded during the summer. But after dark, the long ribbons of car headlights are clearly moving in only one direction. You join the queue, behinds Minis full of nuns, battered country cars in which large men wear caps and the sleek city cars of the suburbanites. Past the new bridge outside Kinsale, the homemade finger marked "Grotto" joins those on the signpost to Garrettstown and the Old Head.

The garages on this quiet road of lush hedgerows and wide views of the river Bandon streaking to the sea, are beginning to stay open late; the shop seems not to close at all, and there at 10.30 p.m., the tour buses idle, waiting for the passengers to make their purchases of chocolate bars and cigarettes.

Food is terribly important at Ballinspittle, as are the raincoats and, to a lesser extent, are the folding chairs known as "Pope chairs" since everybody in Ireland bought one in which to await the helicopter during the visit of Pope John Paul II in 1979. The

Ballinspittle raincoats will have a shorter life, they are all see-through plastic, in purple, green and white, and inside them arms are folded in heavy cardigans or this year's wide-shouldered cotton jackets.

Depending on the night, the cars can be parked bumper to bumper up to two miles from the grotto. It is impossible to turn on the narrow road, now dotted with tour buses, and all the time more people are arriving. You walk down the dark road, passing invisible people, whose presence is manifest only by voices and the crackle of plastic raincoats. "I definitely saw it, but when I put on the binoculars, it didn't move at all." "She kind of sways". "Jesus I'm starving" — There are groups around the open boots of cars; torches illuminating their flasks of tea, columns of sandwiches in bread wrapping and pieces of apple tart in Tupperware boxes. People are hopping up and down on the tyre furrowed verge, easing into welligtons. The stream gurgles along.

Nearer the grotto another sound joins that of the stream; it is the high refined recitation of the Rosary by a lady committee member from over the loudspeaker. The crowds answer in a deeper, more sonorous voice.

There are now two telephone kiosks at Ballinspittle grotto, and two raw concrete toilets. Across the road from the shrine, what was a steep hill of clumped grass, with a busy running stream, ferns, gorse and brambles, is now a naked hillside, covered in sand culled from the seashore. The natural vegetation has been bulldozed away, and the stream covered over. A wide footpath is being laid, and huge prefabricated pipes wait to be buried, to carry off the stream. Always there are thousands in front of the grotto, where a rough sign indicates seating for invalids and old people, and an offering box is chained to a tar barrel.

At the end of each rosary the pace changes . . . "Oh Mary conceived without sin, save us from the fires of Hell. Lead all souls to Heaven, especially those who are in most need of thy mercy . . ." then the Memorare and a cracked and warbled hymn. The crowd relaxes, and there is chatter, some people move off, others arrive. The new County Council street lights provide an unwavering light on the statue and the grotto.

The committee members, who have been working around the clock since last June, are less bumptious now, growing used to the bit of notoriety, they are not as vociferous in their marshalling.

People sit or stand on the hillside, some with binoculars, others, sitting on black plastic rubbish bags in the dark, eat their pilgrims' picnics. There is little noise or giggling though small children run about. The rain of the muggy summer has ceased, and the moon pierces a cold sky. One's breath is a fog in the new chill of autumn. The night is very still and there is no doubt but that the statue is moving. In an erratic motion of head and shoulders, inside the stoney sentry box she jigs, whatever way I screw up my eyes, change position or shake my head, each time I sneak an unbelieving look, the statue is "moving."

I know she is half a ton of concrete — I met the man who made her thirty years ago, in a works in Cork city always known locally as "Chalkey God's." "She's a five foot eight Lourdes," said Maurice O'Donnell matter-of-factly. "Made out of concrete — the indoor statues are usually three foot Lourdes, made out of plaster. Her hands are reinforced with wire, and I remember the day she left the works for Ballinspittle. I was making so many at that time, there was no time to dry them out before painting, so lots of the statues in the shrines around the country are still unpainted. But that was in the Marian year, 1954. The bottom has dropped out of the statues market since the Vatical Council."

I know that a group of psychologists at UCC went to Ballinspittle and said that the statue only *appeared* to move, it was all an optical illusion, it had to do with swaying people standing staring at immobile objects and with auto-suggestion. A committee member and local county council man retorted, furious, that how could the psychologists know — he'd seen their photo on the paper, and sure three of the four of them were wearing glasses!".

I know that the Bishop of Cork, Dr Michael Murphy has urged caution in making claims of movement, and though he did not condemn the nightly pilgrimages to Ballinspittle, neither did he allow Mass there on the Feast of the Assumption.

I know that the ex-Professor of Moral Theology at Maynooth, now parish priest of Mallow, Canon Denis O'Callaghan, finds the visitations to Ballinspittle slightly disturbing, because they speak of a wish for sensationalism in Catholics, and he feels that visits to Ballinspittle could in fact damage one's faith, in a sort of anti-climax way. The greatest mystery of all is the Mass, feels Canon O'Callaghan, but the faithful are staying away from that, and going to worship a statue instead.

Isabel Healy

I know that Blarney guard Jim O'Herlihy went down to Ballinspittle and set up his Olympus camera with zoom lens and flash on a tripod by a tar barrel, and took several photographs of the statue. He saw the statue 'move' but when he looked at it through the lens of his camera it was stationary. He took several photographs, and when they were processed commercially, they showed the hands in different positions. "I can't explain it — and I wish someone would," says Jim. "It just does seem to move, and the photographs though taken from the same angle, with the tripod in the same position, really do show the hands in different positions." Since he took the photos, Jim is getting a fierce razzing from his colleagues — phones ring at the station, and Jim is told "It's God for you . . ."

I am standing in the clear night air, watching a statue jig. Beside me are bus-loads of people on a Pioneer Total Abstinence tour from Kilavullen — they have been on the road for twelve hours. There are people from Mitchelstown and Tralee and Limerick, as well as those who drove the thirty odd miles from town. A child is excited, seeing "movement", but his father hushes his squeals, and continues talking in serious tones about the state of the crops in Tipperary, from where he has driven.

One woman pretends to her friends she sees nothing. There are rumours that the people of Knock are raging because Ballinspittle has taken from their custom. There are no rosary beads or plastic holy water containers on sale here yet, but there are signs outside houses advertising teas and scones, and car park costs £1.

I know it is an optical illusion, but why in heaven's name do we all start seeing it at the same time? The last reason I would venture would be divine intervention, but whoever thought up the idea for getting more than 40,000 people per week to stand in the rain and say incessant rosaries for peace for the past three months — must at least have had divine inspiration.

Monuments On The Move

Eanna Brophy

With virtually every townland and village in the country now reporting monuments on the move and other wonders, I went down to Ballinspittle, Co. Cork last Sunday to view the one which is rapidly taking on the reputation of being the true, authentic, moving statue.

And, yes I did "see" some movement, and I did "see" the face seeming to change. But there were no miracles involved.

It was dusk as I sped south from Cork City; the road that winds down to Kinsale was busy with traffic, some of it no doubt bound for the gourmet delights of that town, but most, as it turned out, following the signs that say simply "Grotto" and lead you out along smaller roads to the little village tucked away among green undulating hills, and fields heavy with the harvest.

A mile or so up the hill from Ballinspittle you meet a diversion sign. It has become necessary, particularly on weekends, to introduce a one-way system to cope with the cars and coaches that bring people in their hundreds to see the statue. After dark is the time when things are supposed to start happening.

As I got out of my car in the village, the first person I spoke to turned out, by pure coincidence, to be one of the teenage girls who first reported seeing the statue "move". She did not want to give her name, because some reporter from an English paper had been talking to her and her friends and had made them look like "right eejits". In fact, she seemed just a little bit fed up with being asked about her experience, but I persevered as we walked towards the nearby line of burger-and-chip vans which were starting to do a roaring trade (50p for a fairly small single). Further along the village street there were ten coaches — some from as far away as Dublin and Limerick.

I asked my modern visionary if she had been thinking holy thoughts or praying at the grotto when the first incident occurred.

25

"Not at all" she laughed, "If I was thinking of anything, it was about the good time we'd had in Cleo's Disco in Bandon the night before."

She and her friends were not going up the road (it's about half a mile from the village) last Sunday night to visit the statue. She had gone back to visit it occasionally — but although scores of other people had seen movements since then, she herself had not. But it had definitely moved that first Monday night when she and thirteen friends were gathered there. "It did move and that's that", she said emphatically. She had drawn no conclusions or messages from the occurrence.

The trees almost form a tunnel over the slightly uphill road to the grotto. It was lined with parked cars and thronged with people, many of them local, but many more from further afield. Among them were family groups in their Sunday best, as well as holidaymakers who came out of curiosity, and the hundreds who had come by coach either for a pilgrimage or a sightseeing trip.

The grotto itself is set in a dark hillside, and surrounded by a well-tended shrubbery. Opposite it is a hillside which was once a field, but now is a roped off enclosure which the feet of thousands of visitors have turned to bare earth. There is a brand new stretch of concrete footpath across the road from the grotto. As I approached, the swelling sound of the rosary filled the night air. There were about a thousand people there, and more arriving every minute.

I went up the hill and looked at the statue, but it seemed too far away. People were sitting on the ground, with binoculars trained on it; others were taking pictures with flash cameras. The statue is in a cave-like setting, with a bright halo of bulbs around its head.

Moving down the hill to stand in the road (which is closed to traffic at night) I heard an elderly woman remark to her friend "'Tis St. Joseph now." It still looked like a statue to me, but I kept on looking. Someone over at the other side of the crowd was leading the rosary through a public address system. I moved to one side of the crowd, to shade my eyes from a street lamp which shone down from another part of the hillside. I was about 50 feet from the statue.

The halo of bulbs was throwing a deep shadow under the statue's chin. As I kept looking, things began to blur a bit, and with a bit of imagination you could say that the shadow under the chin had become a beard. Various people have reported seeing the face of Christ, or Padre Pio, or St. Joseph. And I could see why they would say this: the more I looked at the brightly lit statue, the more it became a strain on the eyes — and everyone there was staring at it too. Naturally the effect of staring at a bright object set in a dark background plays tricks on the eyes. All you need then is a bit of atmosphere and an eagerness to see strange things, and you will.

I found that by tilting my head one way, I could see "the bearded face", but a slight move of the head brought the statue back into proper focus. A young man beside me breathed "She's moving well tonight!" I looked to see if he was joking, but he wasn't: he looked quite excited. This was his first visit here, and he could see a rocking motion. I moved in a bit nearer, and by staring for a long time, produced this effect on my own eyes. Then I looked up at the street lamp and got exactly the same result: the pole which held it began to waver back and forth. Eye strain again.

Between the Hail Marys, people in the crowd were murmuring to each other about what they could see. Some could see nothing at all out of the ordinary, and seemed disappointed. I heard a child tell her mother that she had seen "Our Lady trying to genuflect". A woman told me that she had thought the statue was going to fall out on top of her.

I heard another woman tell a hushed group that she could see "little birds, flying in and out of Mary's crown". I hadn't the nerve to tell her it was moths: you get a lot of them around a bright light of an autumn evening. But a few minutes or so later, I heard another man of about twenty say to a few people "Look, look, there's something definitely moving up around her head!" I mentioned moths to him (I could see them clearly) but he was reluctant to accept a natural explanation.

The prayers and responses rolled on, and people came and went. As I made my way back down to the village, the darkness under the trees was nearly impenetrable, except for the odd headlight as a car turned, or someone approached carrying a torch. As I walked along, listening to voices in the dark telling each other what they had seen, I couldn't help thinking of Kitty the Hare. The tales of Victor O'D Power held great sway of the Irish imagination in the days (and nights) before rural

27

electrification and television. Today, there are many who would like to return to the old certainties of those days, and who long for a sign or message of some kind that help is at hand.

Add that to a bit of optical illusion and auto-suggestion and you have Ballinspittle.

The following morning I went back for a second look. The coaches and burger vans were gone, and there were about thirty people saying the rosary in the sunshine. It was very pleasant. And the statue was just a statue. Still.

The Sunday Press, 15 September.

Did Mary's Statue Really Move?

Peter Kellner

I had to see it for myself. For days the locals in West Cork had talked of little else. The area's daily newspaper, the *Cork Examiner,* had run ever more remarkable stories about it. Then London journalists started descending: Radio Four's 'Today' programme ran a feature, and the *Daily Mail*'s star feature writer, John Edwards, was sniffing the air. From my backwater holiday retreat 40 miles away I decided that I could trust no one's eyes but my own. Did Ballinspittle's life-size stone statue of the Virgin Mary rock nightly of its — her? — own accord from the waist up, or not?

The saga of the statue began about a month ago in this village, 20 miles south of Cork. One evening, at dusk, Clare Mahony was passing Ballinspittle's grotto. She looked up from the road towards the statue, which was about 30 yards away, set in a nook high in the rocky hillside. The statue was illuminated by a halo of eleven lights. As Clare looked up, she was certain that Mary was rocking back and forward.

Clare told her mother and other villagers. They looked. They also saw Mary move. Word quickly spread. A short story appeared in the *Cork Examiner.* People came from other villages to see for themselves. They also saw the statue rocking to and fro. One or two people reported other movements: the twisting of Mary's body, a glint in her eyes, a gesture with her arms.

Within days thousands of people were visiting Ballinspittle nightly, some travelling hundreds of miles, to watch the statue from the road or from the field opposite. From ten each evening on, at 20-minute intervals, prayers were spoken over loud-speakers and most of the spectators-cum-congregation joined in. Seldom in the history of Hail Marys can either the Hails or the Marys have been quite so remarkable. Each night many people left Ballinspittle convinced that they had witnessed a miracle.

29

Two things then happened. First, Ballinspittle became a major provincial Irish news story. When one man with a history of heart trouble died one night as he prayed near the statue, his death became front page news. And second, the church hierarchy became distinctly edgy. Bishop Michael Murphy of Cork warned that "commonsense would demand that we approach the claims made concerning the grotto in Ballinspittle with prudence and caution." But the bishop added: "I understand that crowds are gathering there in a great spirit of prayer. This is certainly a praiseworthy thing."

As I have said, I had to see for myself. One evening I drove to Ballinspittle with my wife, her brother and his wife (both converts to Catholicism and now living in West Cork). Before proceeding to describe what happened, I should perhaps add that the only drink I had consumed all day was a half pint of Guinness at lunchtime.

We had to park the car some 20 minutes' walk from the shrine. It was just after 10 pm when we reached the point where thousands congregated each night. Stewards motioned us to join most of the other visitors by climbing the sloping field opposite the statue. This, however, meant staring at Mary from 50 to 100 yards away: much too far to observe anything clearly. So I explained to the steward that I was a journalist and he let me through to join those at the point on the roadside nearest to the statue — roughly where Clare Mahony had first seen it move.

I then stood and watched, trying to disregard the camera flashes and the wandering torch beams that interfered with a constant, careful view of the statue. (When the cameras weren't flashing and the torches were off, the only illumination of the statue came from Mary's halo. This meant that her head was well lit, her body above the waist moderately well lit, and the lower half of the statue and the rocks immediately behind only dimly lit).

After adjusting for the light conditions, standing as still as I could, and trying to disregard the enthusiastic words of people near me, I came to my first clear conclusion of the evening: *the statue did appear to move* — to rock to and fro, just like the papers had reported thousands of other people saying it did. But why did it 'move'? I was sure it was not, as sceptics had suggested, mass hysteria. Some people may have gone to Ballinspittle wanting to 'see' Mary move. I did not; besides, I am not a Catholic. Either some curious optical effect was at work — or it was a miracle.

Unfortunately, the simplest way of testing whether the movement was real or not was not available. Nobody was able — to be more precise, nobody was *allowed* — to climb near enough the statue to photograph or otherwise record in some way the statue's movement or lack of it. We had to make do as best we could with what our senses told us from a distance.

What made matters more difficult was that the dimness of the lower half of Mary's body and of the nearby rocks made it hard to judge clearly the 'movement' against the statue's fixed surrounds. Could it be that the explanation derived from this contrast between the brightness of Mary's face and the dimness of its backdrop?

Oberving other people staring at the statue I noticed two things. One was that almost everyone was concentrating as hard as possible, trying to keep absolutely still. The second thing was that, even so, nobody managed to keep his or her head absolutely still: everyone's head moved — slightly but constantly. Presumably mine did too. Was this part of the explanation?

To check I exaggerated the head movements I had observed in others: I shook my head just an inch or so from side to side, but very fast. Heaven knows what effect this had on other people nearby. I know what effect it had on me: Mary's head and shoulders appeared to dance furiously. I tried the same thing out staring at a lamp that had been fixed to a telegraph pole, shining out towards the congregation so that they could see where they were going. When my head shook, the lamp also appeared to vibrate against the pole.

I left Ballinspittle certain that the explanation for the statue's 'movement' lay in the optical effects of the way Mary's head was lit. The next morning the *Cork Examiner* confirmed my impressions. It carried a report about a team of psychologists from Cork's University College. They had studied the 'miracle' and confirmed that people standing at night some distance from a brightly-lit object which is set against dim surrounds will appear to see movement: our eyes work best in daylight, and are susceptible to being deceived at night.

Not that the Cork team's findings cut any ice with the faithful. Rumours spread that they had been put up to it by the Bishop of Cork in order to bring his flock back into line. The rumours were denied. And each night, thousands continued to descend on

Peter Kellner

Ballinspittle to watch and to pray. By last week at least 100,000 people had visited the grotto — a sizeable proportion of the population of County Cork and towns and villages in neighbouring counties. As far as I could judge, many of them continued to believe that they had witnessed a miracle.

It would be easy to dismiss all this from the safety of urban, secular Britain as just a quixotic, rural Catholic phenomenon: how odd, how sad, how *silly*. In fact what has been happening at Ballinspittle is very impressive: thousands of people enduring often uncomfortable weather, praying together without any extravagent emotion, leaving hardly any litter. The village provides a far more heartwarming spectacle of people gathering in large numbers than, say, the average English football crowd, or a march through Derry. Except that it is based on an illusion, and surely that renders the whole nightly ritual ultimately meaningless, even dangerous.

Or does it? These are deep waters. Back to politics next week.

New Statesman, 16 August.

A Most Impressive Sight To Behold

Eamonn McCann

A great deal of nonsense has been talked and written about the 'moving' statue in Ballinspittle. The most obvious nonsense comes from those who claim that they have seen the statue move. The statue at Ballinspittle is made of stone, it doesn't move and that's that.

The night I went to Ballinspittle three or four thousand people eventually gathered at the grotto about half a mile outside the village. The grotto is beautifully situated, the statue set about 30 feet up in a natural recess in a hillside. Above and on both sides of the statue are trees and bushes and shrubs, green and olive and russet-brown. The brow of the hill is about 30 feet above the statue. On the opposite side of the narrow road is a field which slopes at a gradiant which would be appropriate to the terracing of a football stadium. Anyone standing anywhere in the field has a clear and unobstructed view of the statue. The field could comfortably accommodate six or seven thousand people. As dusk began to gather the sky above the hillside across the road glowed magenta. A soft wind ruffled the trees and bushes into gentle sighs. As darkness gradually deepened the lighted halo around the statue's head shone out more brightly. Crowds streamed quietly up from the direction of the village to begin to fill up the field. They'd take their stand, hands clasped, and join in the undulating rosary responses. It is certainly a most impressive scene to behold.

When I'd driven into the village earlier in the evening the first people I saw were a gang of Hell's Angles, uniformed in black leather outfits with the logos of heavy metal rock bands on their backs. There was seven or eight of them wheeling and turning and revving their motor bikes noisily. I assumed that they weren't local and speculated that perhaps they'd come to disrupt the proceedings. Later I saw them lined up at the grotto, staring intently across at the statue. They weren't especially reverent, weren't joining in the rosary or in the singing of the Marian hymns which alternated with the prayers, but they were quiet and stood mostly with hands clasped in front of them, and when they left they all blessed themselves before putting their crash helmets back on. When I asked them why they'd come they explained that they often went out for a spin on their bikes in the evening from Cork city and had just decided to take a spin over to Ballinspittle to see what all the fuss was about. None of them believed that the statue really moved.

Meeting the Hell's Angels made me feel easier about the whole affair. I'd assumed that the gathering would be oppressive and quite likely hostile to anyone who was sceptical about the statue moving. The apprehension may have had something to do with my experiences in the North, where there is a largish overlap between religious piety and sectarian hatred. But the gathering at Ballinspittle wasn't like that at all.

Apart from the flock of Angels there were various small groups who one could see weren't exactly in the grip of religious ecstasy. Towards the back of the crowd there were small groups of teenagers, some sitting, smoking and chatting. There were young couples who watched with arms around one another's shoulder and waist. I was stopped twice as I moved through the crowd by people who recognised me and who began conversation by remarking that "Isn't it great crack altogether?" and "By Jesus, you'll get a few columns out of this, did you ever see the like in your life" etc. Such elements were, of course, in a minority. But they clearly felt quite relaxed about being there in a minority.

Of course the majority did appear to be taking the proceedings very seriously — which is not exactly the same thing as believing that the statue really moves. Many had binoculars, a few had cameras, they were praying aloud, their eyes in fixed focus staring at the statue, and they stayed a long time. It is likely that they also took seriously the pitch being made by the man with the microphone who was leading the rosary. He interspersed the decades with pointed litle homilies. He talked repeatedly about "signs". "Our Lady" was giving us a sign. Or the sign was coming from "above". Those who were in personal receipt of these signs were encouraged to "rejoice". He spoke, too, about the "perplexing times" we live in, of the amount of evil that is in the world, of the vulnerability of "our young people" to immoral influence. One rosary was offered explicitly "for all the young people here present that their faith might be strengthened." "Our Lady" was addressed directly and asked to "have pity on your Irish children."

The significance of this seems to me to be perfectly plain. There are many thousands of people in Ireland who desperately want to believe in supernatural signs. Times are, indeed, perplexing. Many things which Irish Catholics have been taught by the Church to believe under pain of mortal sin have been shown to be nonsense. Women have been taught that they would go to hell if they used "artificial" contraceptives. But they know that if they go along with this they'll be prisoners of pregnancy and child-rearing all their active, adult lives. Catholics have been told that divorce is sinful in the eyes of a loving God, but can't see misery and unhappiness all around them resulting from the absence of divorce. The Catholic leaders preach that abortion is the ultimate horror of horrors but a very considerable number of nominally-Catholic people don't accept this in practice — as is evident from statistics showing that young Catholic Irishwomen are just as likely to have abortions as their British counterparts. And so on.

Because of all this, great and growing numbers of people in the 26 county area are no longer able to accept the authority of the Church with blind faith. And in that situation there are bound to be many who, having nothing *but* their religion to comfort them in a cruel world, yearn deep down for a sign that there *is* a supernatural authority which can be relied on. Such a sign, by definition, has to be irrational. Sudden movement by a stone statue of God's virginal mother fits the bill exactly.

This is not speculation. Many of those who claim to have seen the statue move volunteer this explanation. At the grotto field and in the village of Ballinspittle, and over the following few days in Cork, Kinsale and Crosshaven, I spoke to about 30 people who had "seen" the statue move. There was considerable confusion about the nature of the movement. Only one person to whom I spoke — an elderly waiter in a Crosshaven hotel — was adamant that the statue had physically moved and this has been caused by some supernatural agency. *All* of the others admitted the possibility that what they had experienced was an optical illusion. About half believed that optical illusion was the most likely explanation. Some considered no explanation other than optical illusion.

Those who believed it possible that they had witnessed a miracle reckoned that the miracle, if such it be, must mean something. And there was almost unanimous agreement that it meant "Our Lady" or "God" was displeased by the trend of events in Ireland and was indicating that some reversion towards the way things were in the past would be in order. This interpretation would have been encouraged by the musings of the grotto prayer-master and by the fact that the "Virgin Mary' is, anyway, taken to personify sexual — or sexless — purity. However, insofar as one can judge from a series of brief conversations, it did not appear to me that the life-style and practical beliefs of any one of the "seers" had been changed in any way whatsoever by the experience. I met no-one who said: "I used to believe that divorce should be introduced here, but I don't any longer as a result of seeing the statue move" or who said anything remotely approaching this. Those who had previously taken the traditional-Catholic line on these issues continued to take it and quite possible, had been strengthened in their convictions. But those who dissented appeared to continue to dissent. Perhaps the most interesting reaction came from a women in her early 20s who had been leading what Catholic traditionalists would call an immoral life but which is more sensibly seen as having a good, healthy time. She had "seen" the statue move and reckoned that she couldn't rule out the possibility of supernatural intervention. She reasoned as follows: if Our Lady appeared to somebody who is sleeping around, it's clear that sleeping around doesn't cut you off from heaven. The invoking of the Virgin Mary in support of promiscuity may well be an Irish first.

None of those who believed they had possibly seen a miracle appeared to be awe-struck as a result. They talked of what they had "seen" is matter-of-fact tones. "She sort of smiled and looked round to her left," "Her eyes opened and closed and then she nodded," "She made as if to raise her hands up then then she stopped." I gathered no reports of people falling to their knees in wonderment or being transfigured or experiencing any sort of ecstasy. Asked to describe in detail what it *felt* like, most "seers" said that it didn't really feel like anything. They just saw movement. And therein a sense in which it's perfectly reasonable for people to be matter-of-fact about mundane miracles like a stone statue moving. Compared to a belief that a piece of bread can be magicked into the flesh and blood of a man who had been dead for twenty centuries, believing that a stone statue can move is quite reasonable, almost. This is a point which doesn't occur to the "progressive" elements in Dublin who delight to sneer at the supposedly simple-mindedness of the Ballinspittle statue-watchers but who can be counted on to scurry for the safety of their semantic bolt-holes any time a serious frontal challenge is made to the social power of the Catholic Church. The set who confess (privately) that they are athiest, make risque jokes about the pope, think that there is something to be said for the two nations theory, who were on to the Joanne Hayes case as speedily as the females among them were on to electric-pink sweat-shirts earlier this year but who believe that it is inopportune just at the moment to campaign openly for abortion. On the basis of my own visit to the place, I much prefer the company of the Ballinspittle statue-watchers.

The first to see the Statue Move pose in front of the grotto
(photo Michael McSweeney)

I Saw The Virgin Statue Move

Kevin D. O'Connor

Friday August 2. At the Grotto in Ballinspittle. I had come down to this remote part of Cork to report on the strange happenings of the previous ten days.

Phrases in mind: "A boost to the tourist season. The superstitious Irish. Whatever next . . .?"

Still, a reporter is a reporter. The producer of the Pat Kenny Show had asked me, because of my previous reporting of court trials and other 'delicate' stories. In her eyes, I could be relied upon to be 'objective'.

On the car radio, coming down, I had heard an account of another 'moving statue' — in nearby Courtmacsherry. The *Cork Examiner* was quoted as saying such an appearance had usefully coincided with the Harbour Festival.

Lunching with a colleague in Cork, she told me of the folklore already built-up — a local airfield needing a licence and contractors en route with layers of rolled-up tarmacadam.

In Kinsale the first two people I talked to had seen movement on the statue in Ballinspittle. One, a grey-haired woman of calm account, had no doubt. She had the air of an office manageress: "I saw the statue move, from side-to-side." She was a Catholic "but not superstitious." The second woman, on holiday from Shannon Town was equally definite: "I have my beliefs — I saw the statue of Our Lady move."

Was I being set-up? Later, I was to wonder at the power of auto-suggestion, of mass appeal, of group hysteria. In Courtmacsherry, sure enough a small crowd said the Rosary in front of the Grotto which faces onto the sea along the scenic front. And if you did stare at the face long enough, the lighted halo seemed to detach itself. I'm sure it is an optical illusion.

What happened to me in Ballinspittle was different, and unexpected. At 11.30 on Friday night, August 2, I made my way

39

up the climbing country road to the Grotto. Stewards allowed me inside the roped-off area, where detachments from the praying crowds are led to congregate for the duration of a Rosary. Then when I had recorded some recitation of the prayers I left down my recorder.

I absorbed the atmosphere for myself, standing there — with a view to accounting the following morning the mood among the thousands, some in profound piety, knees plunged into the mud of the inclining field opposite The Grotto. Like them I watched intently the features of Our Lady . . .

After a while I felt slowly suffused with pleasure, just watching. The features went out of focus and when they resumed the hands were up to the side of the face, as if she had received a blow. I felt tears come into my eyes at the hurt she was undergoing. She seemed to be passively suffering this pain without protest.

In a kind of trance, but aware of what I was doing, I leaned across to a person next to me and asked if they had seen movement. "No," the girl said. I looked back at the face of the statue and saw further animation. Assuming the girl beside me could see the same, I asked her again if she noticed movement. "No" she said, looking at me a little surprised.

Part of me said: "Look after your job — you're down here to report on this — not to become part of the experience." With some effort I diminished my concentration on the statue, giving up the sensation of pleasure. The face and features had resumed their earlier format, the one familiar to me from seeing the statue first, i.e. with the hands almost joined in prayer motion and the face upturned in that pietistic posture which characterises many statues erected in the Marian Year of 1954.

Fully myself again, I checked I had recorded material and made my way down along the road in the dark. Ahead of me a farming family talked of their experiences. I kept up with them to hear what they said.

I was beginning to doubt what I had seen. Any bias I have is towards scepticism. By the same token, I am aware ". . . there are more things in heaven and earth that are etc."

The family ahead were talking quite matter-of-factly of what they had seen. As they were getting into their car, I introduced myself and asked them to tell me. They told me of movements, in detail. I cannot remember it now but they were a very practical family, the wife in her late '40s, the husband older. Good farming stock. Not the kind of people given to fantasy.

Others to whom I spoke also saw movement. Some did not. There is no rule about it. Some of the pious don't see. Some of the sceptical do. The very uptight and totally resistant probably would not — equally, I suspect, the very pious might not, either.

For my own part, it is no big deal. I do not rule out the 'paranormal' in life. I like animals and nature. All sorts of things go on in those worlds that puzzle me and leave me without explanation.

As did this experience. I make no attempt to analyse or understand it. It happened, that's all.

The Irish Independent, 21 August.

The Moving Statue in Asdee   *(photo Michael McSweeney)*

II

Crowd at Ballinspittle   *(photo Billy MacGill)*

Ballinspittle And The Bishops' Dilemma

Mary Holland

The government press secretary, Peter Prendergast, has now been quoted several times as saying that "three-quarters of the country is laughing heartily" at Ballinspittle.

Daunted by the weather, I haven't visited the shrine, but I have talked to people who have been there and have listened to others describe on television what they believe they have seen. What has happened to them appears to have been a deeply moving religious experience and it is difficult to understand why it should have given rise to such hilarity.

Even to those — perhaps particularly to those — of us who do not share their faith, the crowds at Ballinspittle are a salutary reminder of how divided our society has become in its aspirations, and as such should be a matter of considerable interest to politicians, secular and clerical.

The bishops are not laughing at Ballinspittle, or at Asdee or at any of the other places where people have seen statues of the Virgin Mary move, or watched Christ's face appear, or heard the name of Padre Pio murmured by a plaster image. At the most practical level, such events, and people's apparent need for them, presents the Hierarchy with the immediate problem of what, collectively, its response should be.

The bishops do not want to be seen to encourage superstition, which is why the Bishop of Cork refused to allow a Mass to be said at the grotto in Ballinspittle last week on the feast of the Assumption. On the other hand, as Dr Murphy pointed out, the phenomenon of people coming together to pray is "a praiseworthy thing" from any bishop's point of view, and not to be discouraged, particularly at a time when church attendances generally are dropping.

His comments illustrate the much more general dilemma facing the Hierarchy, which is how to give spiritual leadership to

45

a Church which in Ireland is now quite schizoid in character. How, in fact, can they cater for those who go to Ballinspittle and those who, in Peter Prendergast's words, are "laughing heartily" at it. Since Vatican Two, though by no means entirely because of it, the Catholic Church in Ireland has in the main come to terms with the fact that it can no longer exercise the old, unquestioned authority over its flock.

Half the population is under 25 and subject to far too many influences over which the bishops have no control. In any case, many of their parents have already refused to accept the Church's teachings on such matters as contraception, the indissolubility of marriage or even on what is and isn't a mortal sin.

The liberal establishment, which may be small but is tiresomely vocal, keeps on and on about pluralism, the separation of Church and State, the need to be more generous to Protestants, particularly if the ghastly problems of the North are ever to be resolved.

If all the movement was in this direction, as it has been in some European countries, it would be easier in some ways for the Hierarchy to resolve its problems, at least at a purely pragmatic level. Mass in the vernacular, folk songs instead of Benediction, priests leading demonstrations against President Reagan's foreign policy, a lot of concern about social issues, all these would go a long way towards easing the transition between the old pre-Vatican II authority and a new, more equal relationship between priests and people.

But, as Ballinspittle illustrates, very many Irish Catholics want nothing to do with the new enlightenment and are deeply fearful of the intellectual challenges it presents. They yearn for the old rituals — the Latin Mass, the family Rosary which provided a focus for the evening to which errant children could be summoned, the votive lamp flickering before the picture of the Sacred Heart. It's easy to scoff but these things gave a warmth and comfort to their faith which the new, colder ceremonies have failed to replace, just as the absolute moral authority of the bishops gave a shape and certainty to their lives, now and in the hereafter.

If the crowds at Ballinspittle dramatise the problem facing the Church, the message to the politicans is just as stark. For the yearning after old certainties goes beyond religious practice to reflect an unease with the quality of life in Ireland and with a society which, it now seems to many people, has failed them materially as well as spiritually.

In many ways the shrine at Ballinspittle is the perfect symbol for post-Amendment Ireland. Prior to the Constitution referendum of 1983, it still seemed that socio-political progress on a whole range of issues might evolve quite easily in this country, that we were generous in our willingness to discuss such issues as unwanted pregnancies, divorce, illegitimacy.

The Amendment changed that. At the time a lot of people said hopefully that it wouldn't have a long-term effect, that it was a one-off experience which both sides wanted to put behind them. It was suggested that the full frontal attack from the pulpits in the final weeks of the campaign would be something that the Church would never repeat. I can remember a Fianna Fail TD describing it to me as a kind of moral spasm, powerful because of the emotions which the particular issue of abortion involved, but which would make no practical difference to women's lives.

Since then we have had the death of Ann Lovett and her infant in Granard and the Kerry Babies tribunal, during which it emerged that one of the Hayes sisters had been asked by the police how she had voted in the abortion referendum.

Last week Jane O'Connor, aged 19, was found drowned in the River Dodder at Tallaght. Newspaper reports claimed that she had been bitterly distressed about her pregnancy and felt unable to tell her parents.

We have also had the Bishop of Galway warning doctors in his diocese that the sterilisation of women is repugnant to Catholic Church teaching. Dr Casey felt it necessary to offer this advice when it was discovered that the operation, which takes about 20 minutes, was being performed on women at Galway Regional Hospital when gynaecologists felt there were grave social and medical reasons that merited it. About 100 such operations are performed in the hospital every year.

In the autumn we will have the Society for the Protection of the Unborn Child's case against the Well Woman Centre and Open-Line Counselling, which seeks to stop both places giving advice, including information about abortion in Britain, to women with unwanted pregnancies.

If Bishop Casey's reminders about Catholic teaching are effective, and women cannot have their fallopian tubes tied in a simple operation at Galway Hospital, more of them will come to

Mary Holland

Dublin to try and find out about getting abortions in Britain. If they cannot get the advice and information they require from Irish doctors and counsellors who understand their problems, they will go to England anyway. They will just be a lot more isolated, frightened and lonely.

The government is running scared on all these issues and, in a way, looking at those faces at Ballinspittle, it's easy to understand why. Would you run a referendum on divorce, to take an issue at random, while the Virgin Mary was reminding them and thousands like them that Ireland had remained faithful to the Catholic Church through the worst of the penal days and occupied a special place in her heart?

The Irish Times, 21 August.

Man Does Not Live By Bread Alone

Francis Stuart

"Man does not live by bread alone." Not even by bread and circuses. To put it in more contemporary terms, people have psychic longings that still ache through the thickest layers of material insulation. It does appear, however, that perhaps for the first time in history there are societies, either very prosperous, consumer-orientated or totalitarian ones, in which these needs are either absent or successfully repressed.

The psyche left empty and deprived in a materialist community can be nourished in several ways. In these days and in more sophisticated societies the visual arts, music and particularly literature fulfil this function. Immersed in a world of super-markets, super package-tours, super cars, super sex and the other luxuries, it is not everyone who can find in him or herself the antidote to the commercial propaganda. In countries with a long religious tradition the churches still manage to keep a counter-current flowing and it might well be thought that here in Ireland this is where the Catholic Church would manifest a saving grace. No doubt it does, but to a far lesser extent than it might. For reasons outside the scope of this analysis, the Irish Catholic Church concentrates on moral rather than mystical theology, and a rather limited one at that. Directives on how to vote in referenda about abortion or divorce, sermons and pastorals delivered in the banal language of commercials, constant denunciations of sexual habits and violence, even when justifiable, none of this provides a welcome light in the spiritual gloom.

In fairness, though, it must be said that the Irish are an intensely imaginative but, in general, not a religiously-minded people. We have a great literary tradition, a number of outstanding writers out of all proportion to our size, but little or no tradition of saintliness, despite assumptions to the contrary.

49

From St Patrick to Matt Talbot they have been negative and penitential or loftily aloof. Our patron saint compares poorly with, say, France's when it comes to bestowing inner guidance and comfort. Ste Thérèse of Lisieux is a reality to many people, not only in France, that enriches the inner self and annuls the need for outward signs and wonders.

How bereft of inner or spiritual assurance of any sort must those be who hanker after any public phenomenon that might possibly be miraculous! If at most the miracle-seeker gets a temporary reassurance and a lessening of the feeling of being lost in a cruel and perhaps meaningless world, as with drugs no permanent well-being is provided. Indeed, this sort of 'sign' or marvel is just what could be expected to be hoped for by anyone conditioned in a society that is dominated by material and tangible values. It is sadly in keeping with the way things work, or do not work, in this mechanistic, technological world. If a piece of stone or plaster should move on its own, it would still be a trick or juggling act performed with solid substances and having nothing to do with another or spiritual world. This is so whether the substance is in the form of a holy image or not.

There are occasionally shrines that are a source of strength and comfort to those in distress of one kind or another. But a pilgrimage to Lourdes is not in expectation of witnessing an intervention in Newton's or any other natural law. If an outward miraculous sign was given to Bernadette it was long ago, in verbal form, and never since repeated. Morever, and of vital importance, Bernadette's subsequent life as a nun was an extraordinary one of patience, pain and humility. Instead of watching to catch the slightest hint of something unusual or downright marvellous, the pilgrim there spends time in some degree of meditation or recollection. He or she is not in a condition either of inner emptiness nor even less curiosity.

Nobody need be greatly surprised to hear that one of the statues flew through the air and landed in the next field or on the belfry of the church. Such phenomena have been reliably reported in the past, though usually of pieces of domestic furniture and ascribed to something called a poltergeist, but invariably when neurotics or young people at the age of puberty are around.

Some people feel their very roots in a traditional ground of belief being polluted by the seepage of materialism and scepticism through the land. They are experiencing an acute need for any manifestation that seems to reverse the process. They lack the psychic defences against the constant impact of TV serials, mostly imported, the aggressions of a likewise imported gutter press, and the indiginous advertising with its promise of more fun, more security and more prestige (the worldly trinity), by means of more impressive cars, further afield holidays, bigger and safer insurances, more and better sex.

While feeling a close sympathy for some of those grasping at the "moving statues," they are only adding to the whole superficial scenario or turning up the other side of the tinsel medal.

Many people, writers and artists perhaps more articulatedly, receive from outside their conscious minds intimations of what they believe to be aspects of a reality beyond the sensual, mechanistic world. Many of these are believing Christians who, relying on the message of the New Testament, are convinced they are, however mysteriously, in contact with a heavenly kingdom. In neither case do these channels between one world and the other have anything tangibly miraculous or sensational in the obvious sense about them. Far from constituting an abrogation of any immutable laws they are commensurate with what we are beginning to know of the Cosmos in its basic, if ambiguous, simplicity. Indeed, the kind of hints (to the average person they are something short of 'messages') I am thinking of contain their own power of conviction. In this case the media and the message are truly one.

A desperate need to escape from a sense of inner destitution, that most public and private enterprises and institutions are doing their best to promote, can lead to a superstition that the derangement of solid objects is a proof of the existence of the supernatural. However understandable in the circumstances, it is a fallacy, and indeed, if a sign of anything, it shows how deep in our society has gone the canker of materialism.

Prayer Meeting in West Sligo where a small shrine was erected
(photo Jim Eccles)

Virgin On The Rocks

Nell McCafferty

Given the way the year began it is no wonder that Irish Catholics are flocking by the thousand to Marian shrines where, they sincerely believe, any one of sufficient faith can have a consoling chat with a walking, talking statue of the Virgin Mary. The Lady never mentions sex. She winks and sways morning noon and night, and all through the night, but she has not once invaded the private lives of those who kneel before her.

The year began with two devout adherents of the Catholic faith coming dramatically to public notice, the year was dominated by their separate experiences of private life and Ireland has not finished with them yet. In January, in the county of Kerry, Kevin McNamara was elevated to the most high position of Prince of his Church; Joanne Hayes, his parishioner, was brought before the Kerry Babies Tribunal.

In February, in Kerry, the first statue of the Virgin was seen to move.

For Irish Catholics it has been a year of public weal and sexual trauma that ended in superstitious prostration before the woman who got away — the only earthling ever to have an Immaculate Conception.

Kevin McNamara was promoted to the Archbishopric of Dublin, largest Catholic diocese in all Europe, as a direct reward for his efforts on behalf of Pope John Paul II to stem the flood of permissiveness that both men think is sweeping the Western world. It was from his diocese in Kerry that the once lowly Bishop spearheaded the successful drive to so amend the Irish constitution that abortion, already illegal, would be illegal for evermore. This country is the only one in the world to hold that the fertilised egg is equal in status to the woman who brings it to human fruition within her womb.

Last January, Kevin, now Archbishop, went a step further: all eggs, he said, must be open to fertilisation. He spoke plainly and without ambiguity of any kind. On Irish television he announced that married couples (he recognised no other) for whom natural methods of contraception are unsuitable, should refrain from sexual intercourse. This is the same man who holds that a marriage is invalid if sexual consummation, by which is meant penetration of the vagina by the ejaculatory penis, has not taken place.

Even as this elderly celibate male spoke, his parishioner, Joanne Hayes, a young rural mother, unmarried, was speaking under sedation before an all-male Tribunal of Public Inquiry. She had a baby that died, and the police charged her with murdering another. The Tribunal, ostensibly investigating allegations of police corruption, was obsessed with one single question: could a woman conceive twins by two different men, give secret birth to one in a field, take to her bed and give birth half an hour later to another, which her family then stabs and disposes of, and could the woman all the while silently nurse the fact that there is a small but perfectly formed alibi buried in the field should the police discover the stabbed twin?

"There were times when we all thought she had twins," said Justice Kevin Lynch when the six month Tribunal had come to an end. There were times during those six months when Irish male assumptions about female sexuality touched on the diabolical. "Did she love this man or what he and other men were prepared to do with her?", asked the police counsel about Joanne Hayes.

Even as this lawyer spoke, Kevin Archbishop McNamara was engaged in a trial of strength with the Irish government over which institution, Church or State, should have the right to control women's fertility. The debate that raged between them was described by the media as the greatest political crisis since the fight for independence from Britain in 1916. One parliamentarian summed up the choice thus. "I stand by the Republic," and then he abstained in the vote for the sale of condoms, without a doctor's prescription, to all male adults over the age of 18, irrespective of marital status.

That was the month, February, when statues of the Virgin Mary started walking. The first sighting was in Asdee, County Kerry, birthplace of Jesse James, who went to America and became an outlaw.

Ireland was at "a moral crossroads" warned the former Bishop of Kerry, and "the bitter fruits" of such a policy would be "moral decline, the growth of venereal disease, and a sharp increase in the number of teenage pregnancies, illegitimate births and abortions." He asked how any health board official, claiming to be Christian, could say "I am prepared, if the State so decides, to supply to those who ask the means which will help them to commit serious sin?"

The chief state psychiatrist for his parish of Dublin testified before the Kerry Babies Tribunal that no man had helped Joanne Hayes commit sin. "She got herself pregnant," said Dr Brian McCaffrey.

Other medical men came to the support of their new Archbishop. Seventeen of the country's most powerful senior consultants and doctors warned that the provision of condoms would lead to "an increase in promiscuity with an upsurge in venereal diseases and carcinoma of the cervix."

All the priests in Kerry signed a statement, read out at all Masses, that "artificial contraception and premarital sexual intercourse are always wrong." In the county capital, Tralee, where the mother of 25-year-old Joanne Hayes was asked to account for her "failure to notice that her daughter was pregnant," 11 of the 12 pharmacists continued their refusal to stock condoms.

Justice Kevin Lynch ignored the stand taken by doctors and priests and tried to get to what he saw was the heart of the matter: "Is it possible for a woman to give birth standing up?", querying the insistance of Joanne Hayes that she had given birth in a field. Women have given birth under water, by the side of the road, in aeroplanes, in comas, unnaturally flat on their backs in hospital beds, and even given birth after life had departed their bodies, but this man wanted to know if a woman could give birth standing up.

"、 barefaced, cheating liar," counsel for the police described her.

Defeated, albeit by a narrow majority, on the Condom Bill, the Bishops issued a collective pastoral entitled "Love is for Life." Sexual union, they wrote, is "the means by which a man and a woman say to each other 'I love you . . . I want you to become even more wonderful than you are . . . I need you, I can't live without you . . . I will stay with you through thick and thin'."

This pastoral was read, without a blush, by all the men at all their masses. Also, added the pastoral, extramarital and cohabitional sex were out, as was artificial contraception, homosexuality, euthanisia, sterilisation, abortion even in the case of rape, and not to forget that "God's mercy is there for unmarried mothers who admit their sin and ask His pardon."

Her two parish priests refused to say a cleansing Mass in the family home of Joanne Hayes. Her psychiatrists testified that she did not exhibit "a great degree of guilt at this stage, not as much as I might have thought she would have." Joanne Hayes lives, but other mothers are dying around her, or killing their babies, or casting themselves and their babies on the mercy of strangers and psychiatrists, and adoption agencies and abortion referral clinics.

The months of this sorry year in post amendment Ireland, where it is recommended that all eggs be fertilised, and ordered that all fertilised eggs be brought to fruition under pain of penal servitude for life, have been marked by sad horrors. In a Dublin working class suburb a 19-year-old cast herself and her unborn child upon the waters and drowned; in Northern Ireland a Protestant woman, deserted by her husband, gave birth in the kitchen and stuffed her dead newborn infant in the wardrobe; a newly delivered infant was found by the RUC in a garden; a swaddled baby was found in Galway railway station; a dead baby in a blue pillow cover was found floating in a lake in County Meath; Irish police sealed off a church in Limerick and asked all the women attending Mass to prove innocence of the baby found crying beside the altar; the mental home where Joanne Hayes was temporarily sheltered gave shelter also to the woman who relived, again and again, the shock of sitting on a toilet bowl and rising to find that she had just given birth to a child which fatally cracked its skull on the porcelain.

There has been progress, say some, quoting the Kerry poet who declaimed in verse the true story of his unmarried mentally retarded sister, left in unattended labour in the workhouse, in the hope that such a painful birth would teach her a lesson; that the unmarried mother shall know neither the benefit of hospital nor the mercy of God. She died in childbirth. That, they say, was in 1939.

Joanne Hayes, said a hospital source, had an unexplained voided womb, and the police should check her out as the mother of the stabbed Kerry baby. "You had no intention of allowing that child to leave your womb alive," said the police lawyer about the baby to which she did give birth, which died instantly.

Even as the statues of the Virgin take flight the Bishops have staked out another moral crossroads. In County Galway Bishop Eamonn Casey, he who sang 'Totus Tuus' and 'Stolat' to the Pope, who garners more funds than any other man for the Third World famine, has written to the county hospital authorities. In an open letter he pointed out that the hundred sterilisations performed in 1985 on women who had completed their families ran contrary to God's law as interpreted by Irish bishops. His call for an ethics committee to run the hospital and tell doctors what to do — or not to do — was backed by the hospital consultant, who had also backed the Bishops during the Pro-Life Amendment Campaign.

The Bishops are not crying in the wilderness. Militant lay Catholic organisations whose ranks teem with doctors, nurses and lawyers, have rallied to their cause. Their influence is such that the Minister for Health was recently obliged to reserve 40 out of 200 places in a nurses' training school specifically for Protestant females, in the hope that they would help doctors perform operations which Catholic nurses find repugnant.

Kevin McNamara has allied himself openly with these militant groups. He chose recently to launch a broadside against the contemplated introduction of civil divorce in a speech to Family Solidarity, which sprung up out of the ashes of the Pro-Life forces. Family Solidarity has dual membership with the Society for the Protection of the Unborn Child, and the coalition will this autumn go into court in its sleaziest operation to date, using the name of Eileen Flynn as the trojan horse by which they hope to complete the total occupation of the wombs of Irish women.

Eileen Flynn was a schoolteacher in a rural convent school. She met and fell in love with the father of three children, who cannot under Irish law secure a divorce from the woman who left him ten years ago. Ms Flynn set up home with this man and his children and they had a baby. The courts found this year that the nuns had the right to sack her, not for having a baby, but for conduct contrary to the Catholic ethos of the school. The baby, commented a local priest, was merely "incontrovertible evidence of the immorality of her relationship." In Iran, commented the

Judge, women were stoned to death for committing adultery.

Scarcely had Eileen Flynn packed her bags than SPUC sent a woman claiming to be a pregnant unmarried schoolteacher into the Dublin Well-Woman Centre, which counsels on and caters on all aspects of female health. The woman mentioned Eileen Flynn and said she could not risk losing her job. The centre advised her of all the options open to her, ranging from adoption to abortion. The woman opted for abortion, was given the address of an English clinic, and went straight back to SPUC. SPUC have now taken out a court action, demanding the closure of the Well-Woman Centre, which they say, is an abortion referral centre. The Constitution, they point out, is obliged to protect "as far as is practicable the right to life of the unborn child." It is perfectly practicable to close the Well-Woman Centre.

The desolate situation of Irishwomen was ironically portrayed by a national evening paper on International Women's Day this year. Completely unaware of the significance of the date — 8 March — the paper's front page was entirely devoted to the war of the wombs. The top story headlined the comments of a member of the governing party, Fine Gael: "Escalating social disorder" he said, was due to the fact that "married women are leaving the home to work." Underneath was detailed the case of the unmarried female police officer, suspended from duty for behaviour prejudicial to the good name of the force — she had had a baby. Alongside appeared yet another nugget of wisdom from the Kerry Babies Tribunal: Ireland was a promiscuous society said the detective who secured a false confession of child murder from Joanne Hayes. Many an unsuspecting man, he said, was rearing a child fathered by his neighbour. "It can happen in minutes." Eileen Flynn's appeal against sacking was rejected by the highest court in the land.

That edition of the paper has become a collector's item, offered as a prize in defence fund raffles organised by feminists. Editors meanwhile have chosen to ignore altogether the mumbling of Ireland's moral policemen. Priests, politicians, doctors and lawyers have all been bypassed in favour of a more wholesome story altogether, that of the woman who did it without sexual intercourse, the woman who conceived immaculately, whose lips on the subject are sealed.

The Blessed Virgin does not mention sex. She walks right away from it. She is adored.　　　　　*New Statesman, 13 September.*

Thorn Bushes And Bleeding Statues

Breandán Ó hEithir

The West German film crew, with which I was working, came to Doon Rock, near Kilmacrenan in Donegal, to film the inaugaration site of the O'Donnells, Lords of Tír Chonaill. On a clear day one can see for scores of miles in all directions. But this was mid-September, 1985, and the forecast said that squally showers were sweeping in from the west with only the briefest of sunny intervals between them.

As we waited for one of these we noticed that a number of cars were pulling into the car park below at irregular intervals. The travellers removed their shoes and stockings and performed some simple rites on a patch of soggy marshland nearby. They then knelt at an open well, drank some of the water and rubbed it on their bodies, left some small token of their visit on a nearby bush (an item of clothing, a religious medal, a coin, even a child's soother) and departed.

This is the famous Doon Well and local belief in its healing properties seems to be as strong as ever. The Germans were fascinated. Walking barefoot over marshy ground, kneeling to drink water from an open well from a cracked mug used by hundreds of other pilgrims, as a means of curing illness. They ended by filming much more of the blessed well and the strangely-laden bush than they did of the historic rock.

That night, in the hotel in Dungloe, the young receptionist told us that she often went with her mother to the well. She too believed they had been cured of various ailments after their pilgrimages. Naturally, the conversation strayed to moving statues; the girls in Sligo who claimed to have seen the Virgin Mary and St. Bernadette earlier in the month; and the apparitions at Kerrytown, not far from Dungloe, in the 1930s and 1940s.

The girl was too young to have first-hand knowledge of Kerrytown, but she had heard a lot about the happenings there.

Some still believed that the Virgin Mary appeared on a rock-face there; others were still sceptical. She had heard that the statue near Mount Mellary had spoken and forecast that the world would end on either 28 or 29 September. She was not really amused when I forecast that if that happened the Sam Maguire Cup would forever remain in Kerry.

At breakfast next morning it was decided to include a visit to Culleens in that day's schedule. The village is a mere dot on the undistinguished main road between Sligo and Ballina. Whatever did happen took place on a narrow road that leads off the main road and meanders towards the bleak Ox Mountains. This is close to being the back of beyond; awesome in its remoteness, even at noon on a dull Saturday.

As we rounded a particularly bad bend we saw a pole standing in a muddy field where some cattle and sheep were grazing. In front of the pole, which bore the handwritten legend, "No Talking", two planks were laid on some concrete blocks. There were some ribbons and some battered flowers and nothing else but miles and miles of soggy fields, a scatter of houses and the mountain beyond.

We were soon joined by four cars. One was local, another came from Clare, another from Donegal and the fourth carried a deliciously languorous honeymoon couple from Wicklow. The young bride had been assured by a man in a pub in Enniscrone that the thousands who had knelt in prayer on the muddy site, arose with their clothes as clean as they were when they left home. On his solemn oath they did!

With nervous bravado she went into the field and knelt briefly near the pole. She returned with the knees of her white slacks caked in mud. Round one had the sceptics ahead on points.

The middle-aged couple from Clare kept their own counsel. In Clare you think twice before you crack a joke about Biddy Early's bottle and the misfortunes of the county hurlers. The Donegal contingent sat in the car, with the windows down, whispering and pointing. The woman from Ballina, who was accompanied by a silent husband, told us that she had come there frequently hoping for a spiritual experience, having lost her faith in a benevolent God as a result of two recent, tragic bereavements. So far she had felt nothing; nothing at all. But she had begun to pray again and felt somewhat better for that. She was going to attend the great vigil which was planned for the following day, at which ten thousand people were expected. It was hard to visualise ten thousand people gathered in the middle, or indeed the end, of nowhere. However, we read in Monday's paper that over eight thousand did indeed attend. An RTE reporter showed film of the gathering and reported that he too had felt nothing.

Along the road came one of the four girls who claim to have seen the apparition. She told us her story simply, with the air of someone who is slightly irritated by being the centre of such interest and bored by the constant repetition of the simple facts. They saw the Virgin, accompanied by a figure resembling St. Bernadette, in the sky over the field. They were quite sure. Indeed, they all feel somewhat sorry that this had to happen to them, but what could they do? They only reported what they had seen. What happened since they found somewhat overwhelming. They had decided to come to the field on all the Virgin Mary's feast days.

Everyone is impressed by the girl's straightforward simplicity. She allows the crew to film an interview with her, tidies up the area around the pole and goes home again. As we drove away the four Donegal pilgrims enter the field together and kneel in prayer in front of the pole. I notice that they kneel carefully on the planks. It is now after two o'clock and more and more cars are turning off the main road: first left after the mobile chipper and the sign that reads "Prayer Field".

The director has just published a hefty tome on the subject of hysteria, but when I suggest a small detour to Knock she implies that they have quite enough material on Irish superstitions, ancient and modern, and that Captain Boycott's house is next on the shooting schedule.

But we talk about Kerrytown, moving statues, medicinal marshes, prophesies of impending disasters, and other mysterious phenomena which seem to occupy the minds of so many Irish people. I do my best to keep my lone end up by noting that another German writer, Eric von Daniken, who, in an otherwise worthless book on the supernatural, has compiled "a calendar of visions" from all over the world. Out of the seventy-odd visions recorded between 1900 and 1974, only the Kerrytown vision is credited to Ireland. Not a word about Templemore. Not a word about Ardboe. But even in the middle of World War 2 the Virgin Mary appeared to sixteen year old Barbel Ruess, at Pfaffenhofen, at least a hundred times over a period of six years.

Kerrytown is a hamlet, containing about ten homesteads, near Annagary in the Donegal Gaeltacht. With the exception of Knock it is the only Irish apparition which has been treated seriously in print. A 24 page pamphlet, written in anger and for private circulation by someone with the initials J.R.M., was the result of a brief conversation between the author and a priest from the Diocese of Raphoe.

In July, 1976, in reply to a question about the statues of Kerrytown as a place of pilgrimage, the priest replied, "There never was a Kerrytown. There is no Kerrytown now. There never will be a Kerrytown". This led J.R.M. to set out the facts of what happened on the night of 11 January, 1939, when after a game of cards in the Ward household, various members of the family saw what they took to be the Virgin with the Infant Jesus in her arms, on the face of a large rock near their house.

The news spread and people began to come to Kerrytown, some travelling long distances to pray at the rock at night. There were further apparitions and a report from a local correspondent appeared in *The Irish Press*. Soon, pilgrims were travelling to the remote village from Dublin, Cork and Belfast.

The Parish Priest, Fr McÁteer, first refused to come to Kerrytown to inspect the rock and question those who claimed to have seen the apparitions. Then, remembering, perhaps, that the Parish Priest of Knock refused to go out to see the apparition on the gable end of his church, at the behest of his housekeeper (she was known to be fond of the local poitín), Fr McAteer went to Kerrytown and wrote this account of what he experienced:

"Suddenly, I saw a portion of the Rock become marble white: it was heart-shaped and about 12 feet in diameter. This made me stop. Immediately, there came from the North, over the Rock, on my left, a gold-coloured fiery cloud. In front of the cloud, at the foot of it, stood the Majestic Lady, clothed on the outside in a white garment, and, inside this, from the waist up, in blue. Her hair was hanging down her shoulders as in Murillo's picture of the Assumption and her head was posed sideways towards Her right shoulder. She was looking partly in my direction and her look was one of exceedingly severe censure. The impression I received was that She almost asked me in words: 'Now do you believe?' I could not explain the sensation I felt, and, without knowing it, stretched out my arms, shut my fists and cried out 'Oh! Oh! Oh!' The apparition was so real that I thought that everybody must be able to see it."

Not everyone present that night saw what Fr McAteer described, but some did and afterwards, when the news spread, visitors to Kerrytown became even more numerous and persistent. The fact that the priest had searched for magic lanterns and found none, and that a portion of the Rock was sent away for analysis, to see if there could be some scientific explanation for the lights and images, helped to convince those who wished to believe in a genuine apparition that Kerrytown would soon be a rival to Knock.

But although the Rock continued to be a place of pilgrimage into the 1950s (some people still visit the place today) the church authorities, local and national, gave it no credence and used their influence to stop local newspaper coverage. Still, in 1949, among the visitors to the Rock were Cardinal Dalton, Cardinal Griffin from Britain, and Archbishop Walsh. Cardinal Griffin spoke at length to Minnie Ward, one of the first to have seen the image on the Rock, but gradually Kerrytown faded into folklore and is now largely forgotten outside Donegal: except for one curious thing . . .

It was assumed locally that Our Lady came with a warning for the people. At the end of his pamphlet J.R.M. appends this chilling list, under the heading "Tragedies in the Rosses":

1943 On May 10th, a mine floated into Ballymanus Bay, exploded, killing 19 men and boys, between the ages of 15 and 34.

1960 On November 22nd, three of a crew of six were drowned when their boat struck a rock off Owey Island.

1975 On January 7th, the trawler "Evelyn Marie" sank off Rathlin O'Beirne Island. The crew of six perished.

1976 On November 22nd, the "Carrig Una" foundered off Rathlín O'Beirne Island. The crew of five perished.

After that it is refreshing to turn to the Apparitions of Ardboe, near the shores of Lough Neagh, in Co Tyrone. These happenings, shortly after the end of World War 2, are recorded only in a series of anecdotes; many of them both irreverent and hilarious.

I am sorely tempted to leave them all unrecorded, for I notice that some of them have been improved and embellished over the years. One will suffice to give the flavour of this occasion, after which we shall pass on to more serious matters.

The apparition first took place near a white-thorn bush in the corner of a field. One morning, shortly afterwards and before the huge crowds began to arrive daily, a farmer who was passing by noticed that the bush was gone. A neighbour came by and provided the answer.

"A parcel of cunts from the confraternity of Ardoyne came down last night and took it away with them."

It was later said that the bush was cut up into small pieces, glued to postcards and sold for as much as half a crown apiece to the gullible, as "Genuine Relics of Our Lady of Ardboe." This story and others may well be as fraught with invention as our next case history: the Story of the Bleeding Statues of Templemore.

In the course of my wide-ranging researches I have come upon only one book which contains a reference to the events that stirred Templemore and the whole of Ireland during the second half of 1920.

According to newspaper reports, a 16 year old youth from Curraheen, between the town of Templemore and the Devil's Bit, had a vision on the night of 5 July, 1920, and came into the town where he lodged with an uncle-in-law, Thomas Dwan, a newsagent. Many things were happening in the town at the time. On the night of 17 August, District Inspector Wilson was shot by the IRA and the Black and Tans went on the rampage. In *The Irish Times* of 23 August, buried away among reports of murder and carnage, is a story about a statue in the house of Thomas Dwan which bled during the night. The following day newspapers carried a story headlined, "Prelates Counsel Caution". Templemore became a centre of attention for reasons far removed from the "Troubles".

Patrick Shea, whose father was an officer in the RIC in Templemore at the time, gives his account of the happenings. According to him, the Blessed Virgin appeared to young Walsh (who had been a member of a religious order for a period, before returning to Curraheen) and told him of her displeasure at the sinful happenings in Ireland. At her request he had scraped a small hole in the floor of his house and the hole had filled with water that became a running spring well.

On 8 September, advertisments appeared in the Dublin evening papers to announce the opening hours for the Holy Well at Curraheen: 10 am - 4 pm Irish Time. By this time the Templemore Miracles had become a national attraction. The Great Southern and Western Railway ran their first Sunday excursions since the war; 13/- 3rd class return. The first train left 800 behind at Kingsbridge and 14 extra coaches had to be procured.

The miracles were many and various; ranging from a British soldier who was converted to Catholicism after seeing a vision of the Blessed Virgin on the roof of Templemore Courthouse, to a child whose tubercular leg was cured. Archdeacon Ryan of Cashel denied that any miracles had occurred. However, the crowds got bigger and bigger and bottles of water from Curraheen holy well were fetching high prices all over Ireland. Notices appeared in the Dublin evening papers announcing the departure times for charabancs from O'Connell Bridge to Templemore, daily.

But despite all the excitement and the publicity, by December the Templemore affair was as dead as the dodo. Clerical pressure, particularly on the press locally, contributed to its decline; but there were other reasons. Patrick Shea describes how a cripple in the town was cured after touching the blood-covered statues which were placed on a table in front of Mr Dwan's shop. The Cashman collection of photographs contains many pictures of the vast throngs kneeling in front of these statues. He also describes the arrival at Templemore Barracks of a woman who had travelled from Donegal with her deformed child.

She had tried in vain to get to the holy well. She had failed also to get near the bleeding statues in Mr Dwan's yard, but had heard that a statue which a constable in the barracks had purchased from Mr Dwan, was found to have been covered in blood when taken from its container. She and hundreds of others laid siege to the barracks, demanding access to the statue. The Divisional Commissioner for Munster appeared, on a tour of inspection, and instructed that the blood-stained statue be displayed for the clamouring throng, who then filed past under the supervision of the RIC and the local Black and Tans and military.

To explain the sudden end of the Templemore affair is really to explain its sudden beginning. Nobody really knows what it was all about, and those who think they know are wisely silent. For far away in Australia is the "Saint" Walsh; one hand on his Rosary beads and another on a sheaf of writs to be let loose on any infidel who might insinuate that the bleeding statues of Templemore were anything less than what they seemed to be at the time; not to mention anything more.

Patrick Shea maintains that the IRA took full advantage of the affair to distribute guns and ammunition, as well as men. The huge crowds of pilgrims (for want of a better word) made a total mockery of the regulation which prohibited motorists from travelling more than 20 miles without a permit.

They may have benefitted in more practical ways also. However, as one who ran the gauntlet of Templemore silence — of a most aggressive nature — on the subject of the 1920 miracles, let me counsel caution. Nobody in the town, or in its immediate vicinity, wants to be reminded of this strange episode in Irish social and religious history.

I think I know what happened. I have a fair idea of why the proposed statue to the converted Black and Tan was never erected. I have read all the contemporary newspapers and met some of the people who did not attend the school but who certainly met the scholars. And after all that I will only say this: Templemore would knock Kerrytown, Ardboe and Knock itself . . . yes even Lourdes . . . into a cocked mitre. More than that I am not willing to say: wild horses wouldn't drag it out of me.

A Manifestation Of Popular Religion

Dáithí Ó hÓgáin

There are several surprising things about the debate we have been listening to for the past while. Not least is that the subject of the statues is discussed in isolation, as if it had no need to be related to contingent cultural circumstances and indeed to tradition in general. Those who are disposed to accept the phenomena as miraculous tend to see this very isolation as being proof of its supernatural force. The whole point, after all, is that God, and particularly the Blessed Virgin, are drawing attention to the chaos of contemporary life and wish their intervention to be noticed.

On the other hand, journalists and commentators in general are having their eyes opened to deep divergences between their own perception of the world and that of large numbers of the public. They react to this by trying to experience the world as the devotees of the statues do, with the result that instead of getting a comprehensive insight into the question, they run the risk of either condemning the proceedings outright or else swapping one closed perspective for another.

The third approach which is adopted is the scientific one, and there is no doubt but that individual disciplines can shed some light on what is happening. The statements of ophthalmologists, for example, appear to have value in the context. An in-put by sociologists would also be welcome, for many observers suspect — and some openly state — that changing life patterns, as well as some recent controversies associated with these, are contributory factors. The present writer, however, feels that in order to get a good overview of the whole situation, one definite area needs to be examined and assessed. This is the background in culture and tradition.

The first premise of my argument will be readily accepted by people of whatever persuasion regarding the matter. That is, that statues are in themselves a rather unique aspect of culture. Researchers in many parts of the world and in widely different civilisations bear witness to the tendency which people have to give extra force and significance to statues above other types of symbols. For a statue not only signifies the idea or spirit in question, but it also represents it down to the minutest detail which its sculptor could attain. A statue, therefore, in directing our attention to what it signifies, can also be seen as in a special way embodying it. In the sphere of religion, this quality is enhanced by another facet of human perception — the tendency to regard certain objects as sacred, since they are media through which we come into contact with the ineffable. This is the crux of the long-running battle in religious history between iconophily and iconoclasm — devotion to statues and images versus hostility to them. When relating this general background to the Irish situation, it is well to remember that the Roman Catholic Church has always cautioned against regarding statues or paintings as being in themselves sacred. Rather are they to be regarded as conventional ways of drawing people's attention to the sacred.

Yet it must be admitted that a statue in itself invites speculation concerning the figure represented. It is an image of the hero or saint or deity, and from it one can see (through the skill of its maker) the actual appearance of that personage. To the eye of the beholder it is a substitute for the body — a substitute which equates to the visible appearance of that body. Furthermore, it is intended by the artist to convey the significance of the personage. In other words, just as the body encompasses the personality, the statue can be felt to encompass the significance. To the devoted beholder — especially when experiencing strong subjective rapport with the lauded one — the dividing line between these two sets of relationships can become very thin. As significance shades into personality or even soul, the statue can be pictured as the body, and the lauded one is expected to react in a physical way to the devotee.

The idea of statues coming to life, or at least showing enough signs of life to vindicate the trust of the devotee, is an old and widely-attested one. It existed in ancient Egyptian religion, where oracles were wont to be given in this way. A statue of the god was brought out in procession and important issues of state were placed before it. It answered "yes" or "no" to the queries by supposedly moving backwards or forwards. No doubt the principle of "like influences like" was at work in such cases — many peoples in both ancient and modern times have had the feeling that a well-executed image can apportion to itself the power of the original person or thing. The consummate skill with which some sculptures were done in itself helped to strengthen these ideas, for the true artist was believed to be gifted with genius from the otherworld. There were thus a combination of ideas regarding why some special statues, or paintings, were believed to have supernatural import. Such attitudes were carried over into Christendom, and we find that many images of the Blessed Virgin were traced back to supernatural sources.

From the early Middle Ages onwards, hundreds of statues and pictures of Mary were reputed to have been carved or painted by the Evangelist Luke, acting under divine inspiration, and several others were attributed to the hands of angels themselves. This entailed, in the popular mind, the possession of divine energy by the images; and so mediaeval Christianity was replete with legends of how statues of the Virgin wept, shed blood, moved head and arms, and in general intervened in this world to assist sinners and vindicate Christian belief. One particularly beautiful account tells of how a street acrobat became a monk, but so ill-educated was he that he could not join in the prayers at the monastery. So, in place of this, he went every night and performed his tricks in front of a statue of Mary, thereby honouring her in the only way he knew. The abbot became suspicious, and he hid in the crypt one night to see what the ignorant monk was up to. After a long session of tricks and tumbling, the poor monk fell exhausted at the statue's feet. Then the abbot saw the Blessed Virgin herself step down from the pedestal and gently wipe the sweat from her servant's brow with a cloth.

The predominance of the Madonna in so many forms of popular Christianity raises issues of tradition and derivation which we cannot go into here, but it is clear that goddesses of Egyptian, Greek, and Roman origin had an influence. Indeed, in the south of Europe, old statues of these goddesses often did duty as Mary in Christian churches. Not only did the Blessed Virgin take over the place of these other female deities, but she took over their function as well. Embedded deep in human psychology, the devotion to mother-symbols ensured a very special emphasis for her at all times, and it does so still. By many artists and visionaries, both old and new, she is represented as interceding for doomed humanity, calming the just wrath of her Son and staying His hand from destroying the world. A conversation with people during a prayer-session at the current shrines of moving statues will bring the selfsame ideas to light. There is nothing novel about all this, though it may surprise some of us who think that the past, once left behind, is left behind forever.

The Romans of pre-Christian times had, as archaeology shows us, a great tradition of sculpture, and it is not surprising to find that they also imputed a kind of life to some of their famous statues. One striking legend tells of how a young man once placed a ring on the finger of a statue of Venus. The marble hand closed on the ring, and when he later married an ordinary lady the statue flew into a terrible vexation. Mediaeval Christian scholars rationalised this in support of celibacy — a man who had made a vow to the Virign Mary should devote himself to no other woman. One aspect of the Roman tradition is of particular importance here. This was the idea of prodigies, of signs which portended great changes or great disasters. These included extraordinary visions seen, the appearances to particular people of gods and goddesses with relevant messages, strange phenomena like blood-coloured rain falling from the skies, and statues falling flat on their faces in order to show the displeasure of the deities they represented. When added to Christian apocalyptic, these prodigies and their accompanying prophecies had even greater vogue.

It is interesting to note that demonstrations by images of Our Lady tend to have much of this atmosphere about them. Indeed, the whole tradition of her intercession on the behalf of threatened humanity seems to have derived principally from the celebrated Apocalypse of John — arguably the most influential of all Christian writings in the context of popular Christianity. The vast bulk of people, and of clergy also, took a type of literal and extended meaning from this work and the result has been quite dramatic. Again and again down through the centuries, large numbers of people — daunted by the difficulties of their time and dispairing of any rational solutions — have eagerly awaited and in some cases tried to precipitate the promised divine intervention in our affairs.

The great renewal to be sought after, so the claim goes, is one which is brought about by means not hitherto used or experienced by man. In fact, the basic idea is that man cannot solve his own problems and must abandon his fate totally to the hoped-for, yet feared, events. The reader of mediaeval European history is astounded by the frequency and intensity of such thought and the spontaneous strength of the movements it gave rise to. Lacking a programme, each outburst of emotion soon shot its bolt, to be replaced in time by another and largely identical social phenomenon. The sheer desperation of some of these movements takes our breath away when we consider — admittedly in the role of external and retrospective sages — their confusion of thought and their lack of real prospects. The best-known example is that of the Children's Crusade in the 13th century, which was surrounded by alleged miracles of all kinds but which ended up in total and inglorious disaster. The theological difficulties in such apocalyptic thinking are obvious, and ecclesiastical institutions have generally treated it with great suspicion, if not with total repudiation. But it is important to draw attention to one perennial aspect of apocalyptic ideas in the popular tradition of Europe. That is, that these ideas have very rarely been based directly on the ordinances of church authorities, but have rather developed from independent popular perception of religious tenets. Thus, when pressures come to bear on official religion, thereby causing stress to be laid on certain topics, once this stress is experienced by the populace at large some very definite (and differentiated) folk formulations of the crisis tend to emerge. The distance between these folk formulations and the official ones offers a parallel to what we said above regarding image-interpretation in Christian worship.

The parallel is borne out by some other instances of moving statues. In 1524 Italy was over-run by French forces and Rome itself threatened, floods, famine and plague had brought the people to the point that they considered it the most deplorable epoch in all history. Then a 'miracle' was witnessed by thousands of people at Brescia. They saw a statue of Our Lady open and close its eyes, join and separate its hands with an expression of gravity and sympathy. This was immediately followed by similar visions in other Italian towns. Once the crisis had passed, however, the sightings died away. Moving on in time, a like occurrence took place at Venice in 1716, after the Turks had declared war on that city. A certain man claimed that the Blessed Virgin had appeared to him and stated that if sufficient prayers were offered for the souls in Purgatory victory would be gained over the infidels. A great crowd of people gathered to a church where a statue of Our Lady stood and saw it open and close its eyelids in approval of what the man had said. Both the bishop, and the city's senate, soon afterwards declared their support for the verity of this 'miracle'.

All of this was as nothing, however, compared to the events which occured when the Papal States were under threat from the French revolutionary armies in 1796-97. All over Rome, and spreading to other parts of the country, statues of the Blessed Virgin were seen by people to open and close their eyes, give alternate glances of sadness and consolation, and to shed tears. A papal commission was set up, over nine hundred witnesses were examined, and the resultant report was favourable. When Bonaparte entered Ancone, he rather characteristically ordered the the statue of Mary in the Cathedral there — famed for its movements — to be covered. This singular act had its effect, and reported sightings soon faded away at all the locations. It seems that some senior clergymen had cultivated the belief in this case for political reasons, but an interesting aspect of the whole episode is that the papal commission did not deny the integrity of some witnesses who said that they had watched for prolonged periods but had not seen the statues move.

Statues were not to the fore in Christian worship in Ireland until the last hundred years or so, and so the idea of moving statues seems to be a new one in this country. There is, however, evidence of somewhat similar apocalyptic episodes. A good example is furnished by the events of one week in the year 1832, at a time when cholera epidemics were common and much dreaded. This lasted from 9 June to 15 June, during that time encompassed most of the country, and then subsided as quickly as it had arisen. It consisted of people passing on pieces of turf to each other, this being — it was claimed — the only way to prevent a devestating outbreak of the disease. The activity commenced in Co Cork, and it was related that the Blessed Virgin had appeared to a man at the chapel in Charleville and had left some ashes on the altar there. She said that these ashes were the only protection against cholera, and directed that small packages of them should be placed under the rafters of houses. The head of each household should then take four parcels of ash from his chimney and hand them on to four neighbours. So the passing from hand to hand of the singed turf became general. Two aspects of this movement deserve special notice. One is the apocalyptic sense which pervaded it. As the scare spread, it took on new dimensions of imagery — in most cases it was an impending plague which was expected, in others a striking comet, the curse of God or of some senior cleric, a horrific outbreak of fire, and so on. The second important aspect is the belief that the Blessed Virgin could save the people. Here again, we see her in the role of interceder and proctectress from otherwise overwhelming forces. The same great mother who is the refuge of the sinner at the hour of death is the refuge of the whole community when it is under threat.

It is easy to relate that kind of perspective to some popular feeling in current times. The greatest threatened disaster of all, of course, is that of thermonuclear war; and in recent years the possibility of such a war has gradually come home to everybody. The "sense of an ending" — which many thinkers have identified as prevalent in 20th century thought — has on this account been sharpened and accentuated in the past decade or so. But there are other, more localised, reasons which one suspects are contributory to the rise of a form of apocalyptic thought in contemporary Ireland. Recent years have seen a great barrage of attack on attitudes traditionally held, and this was naturally caused a deal of anxiety. There is the political crisis, and the powerful voices which declare that the age-old Irish struggle against imperialism is tainted and sinful. The failure of this paradigm when applied to the real situation has caused disquiet and no small amount of confusion.

But at least that argument is an old one, and the moving statues of Munster are more closely connected with another and more novel area of confusion. This concerns the assault on traditional mores of sexual conduct by consumerist culture. An objective evaluation of this culture, and of its source in multinational capital, is quite outside the range of education currently available to people, and so it is felt rather than analysed, feared rather than outmanoeuvred. As we said above, popular religious expressions tend to retain and develop elements of official preaching which have been superseded at that level. They can also retain and develop some oblique or incidental references in official preaching and then fill in the gaps. Most people, and some clergymen, do not find it feasible to rationalise abstract ideas, so it is the emotions which are made to carry the burden.

Accordingly, striking and noticable phenomena are felt to buttress the ideology. Prodigies of earth and sky are best suited to this context. Thus we find that prophetic statements like "when the winter becomes summer and the summer winter," "when disaster falls from the heavens", are common among devotees of the moving statues. Rumours of approaching meteors and news of shattering earthquakes add to the atmosphere. Above all else, minds of devotees are haunted by the "secret of Fatima", which is widely believed to refer to some atrocious and world-shattering disaster to come.

The cynic, of course, will have plenty of rationale at his disposal in order to disprove and discredit rumous of moving statues, both in a physical and a moral sense. He can claim that those who have sunk into a hopeless lethargy need prodigies for their own reassurance. This is clear from many popular attitudes, for example the idea of sainthood. To say that a saint is an ordinary person like the rest of us may be good theology, but it makes for bad drama. Likewise with the idea of a miracle. Why ignore the latent miracles which lie in all the world around us, and particularly in the virtue and self-sacrifice of people? Why must a miracle stand out above and beyond all bonds of nature to be noticed, especially when its only purpose seems to be to act as a curiosity? The answer again seems to be "for its dramatic value". But all this is to ignore the basic element in these rather spontaneous movements — the element of personal needs being satisfied within group consciousness, and the concomitant necessity to find meaning in life when such meaning is not otherwise available. This, of course, is the whole point of ritual — of the type of formalised proceedings which people, whether religious or not, find attractive at many levels.

So it is difficult to argue that spontaneous ways of expressing the same needs are less justified than planned and calculated ways. Unfortunately, however, the debate is unlikely to proceed along these lines. Ultimately, most people — from both sides of the fence — will insist that the only important point is whether statues really move or not, whether or not these prodigies are a reality. It would seem to be of far greater value if we searched for the underlying causes which lead people to notice such things at some times and places rather than at others. But defining the search could be just as ambiguous as the original question!

III

The four girls who saw the apparition retracing their steps during a novena (photo Jim Eccles)

A Remote Field In West Sligo

Tommie Gorman

It is the seventh night of the vigil, Sunday 8 September, Our Lady's birthday. Word of the events at Carns is spreading through the country and as many as ten thousand are gathered in the darkness.

The four girls, dressed in either black jackets or capes, are together in the field near the wooden post where the loudspeaker is mounted. They have been leading the prayers and hymns and they pause for a brief rest. In the crowds someone is shouting: "I saw her, I saw her."

A nun takes hold of the microphone and sings. Voices rise up, the curious alongside the puzzled and the devout:

> *Happy birthday to you*
> *Happy birthday to you*
> *Happy birthday, Our Lady,*
> *Happy birthday to you.*

Kathleen Conmy's grazing field at Carns, Castleconnor is a desolate spot. Tuffy's, the nearest pub, is three miles away; it's four miles west to Castleconnor church and a mile south to Kate Boland's shop. Behind, the Ox mountains rise and further off there's the peak of Nephin. Ballina, the nearest big town, is a fifteen minutes drive and the main road, linking it to Sligo is two miles, due south. The surrounding countryside is sparsely populated by small holders who make a living from mixed farming.

On the night of 2 September, a Monday, the stillness at Carns was broken by the murmer of five girls singing. Patricia McGuinness is 15; she wants to be a photographer. Alongside her was 14 year old Colleen, one of her six sisters; her third cousin, Mary McGuinness; and another neighbour, Mary Hanley, at 16 the oldest among the group.

With them was a grand-daughter of Kate Boland, on holidays from England. They were walking her home to the shop through the darkness.

The moon was nowhere to be seen and as the girls passed Conmy's field they were frightened. They were singing "We are the world, we are the people" but here they switched to hymns. They talked of the foolishness of schoolpals who hitch lifts at night, and through the music and chat the anxiety dissipated. At Boland's they said goodnight to their English friend, Diane, and bought bars of Whole Nut chocolate for the one mile walk home. It was unusual for the four to be on the road at this late hour, 10 o'clock. They had gone around in a group since their days in Stokane, the national school, three miles away, run by lay teachers. They like listening to pop music and on television they follow Top of the Pops, Coronation Street and Dallas. That very day Mary Hanley remarked how nothing ever happens in Carns.

As they passed along the lonely road for a second time, at the gate to Kate Conmy's field, Mary Hanley gripped the cape of Colleen McGuinness.

"Look up" she said, "it's her."

Instinctively Colleen's eyes turned skywards and there she saw Our Lady. She was wearing a white veil and her hands were concealed in it. Her face was pale and sad.

To the right of her head was a star and to one side was Saint Bernadette. Mary and Colleen recognised both figures from pictures they had seen. At first the remaining two girls thought Patricia and Colleen were laughing or crying but when they looked up, they also saw an apparition. The Blessed Virgin was about 12 feet in length and she and Saint Bernadette followed the four frightened girls until they came near to Hanley's house.

Josephine Hanley was at the door, letting out a visiting neighbour when she saw her only daughter, Mary, with her three friends, approaching.

"Look" she said, "they're shining."

All four were in an agitated state. They explained to their families how they had seen the Blessed Virgin and they were frightened. That night Mary Hanley was too afraid to sleep in her own home. Instead she stayed with Colleen who had been alongside her when the apparition first appeared, and Colleen's cousin, Mary, also stayed. Patricia McGuinness was content to spend the night with her other sisters. Her father was away from home on business but she would tell him of her experience as soon as he returned the next day.

Patrick McHale was a busy man on the following morning, Tuesday, 3 September. He is the boyfriend of Colette McGuinness whose two sisters, Colleen and Patricia, had viewed the Blessed Virgin over Conmy's field. That next day the girls sought out their local priest, Fr Martin Halloran, and Patrick gave them a lift in his car. On the first visit the parochial house at Castleconnor was empty so the girls asked to be brought to the convent of Jesus and Mary, at Enniscrone, six miles away.

Patricia, Colleen and Mary McGuinness are all pupils at the school, run by Mercy nuns, and they were anxious to tell their story to the Principal. When, after knocking on the main door, they were informed she was busy, they sought out another nun, Sr Maureen McDonagh. A staff meeting was in progress but Sr Maureen left it for a time to talk with the girls. They recall how she seemed to believe them as they told of the previous night's apparition. She told them that they should pray and this also was the advice of a second nun, Sr Emer, when the girls talked with her elsewhere in the convent. It was suggested that they should retrace their footsteps along the route from Boland's shop, past Conmy's field, to their homes.

Still there was no sign of Fr Halloran's car in Castleconnor and Patrick agreed to drive the girls to another school, Gortnor Abbey, thirteen miles away in Crossmolina. Here the last of the four, Mary Hanley, was soon due to return as a boarding student. When Sister Dolores was told of the previous night's experiences, she too seemed delighted and the girls were advised to pray for peace in the world.

It was Patrick McGuinness, the father of Patricia and Colleen, who eventually brought the four girls to Fr Halloran that afternoon. On hearing the accounts when he returned home, he immediately sat the girls into his car. He waited outside while the girls talked with their priest. They were in the living room, sitting down; they got the impression that Fr Halloran was believing them. Once more they were advised to pray further.

Things began quietly. No more than thirty locals were gathered in the field at Carns at 9.30 p.m. on Tuesday, the night after the apparition. As advised, the girls would make the journey on nine successive nights. Some among the small pocket of people had rosary beads and carried torches. Even the sceptics were aware how the four girls were not in the habit of making up daft stories.

It was a quarter past ten when Our Lady appeared to them for the second time. Her face was in the moon. To the right was a headless statue, coloured blue, the shade that's sometimes on the ribbons holding medals worn by altar boys. The girls were looking up at her and this time they were not afraid. They saw her miming what they made out to be the words 'Faith and Hope!' When they recited the prayer 'Hail Queen of Heaven', she continued to mime with them.

Up to thirteen of the crowd present were convinced that they had shared in the vision. Sisters of Patricia and Colleen McGuinness were among them. Some of the girls were lucky but others saw nothing.

Accounts of the supernatural were passing through the parishes in the West of Ireland. One man with mixed feelings was the farmer who had rented Kate Conmy's field. The flow of intrusions by human feet was trampling fences and damaging the quality of grazing land, already poor after the wettest summer since records began. It took a visit from the girls to appease him and the important site in the apparition story was open to the public once more.

It took the third set of visions by the girls on Thursday, 5 September to boost the attendance to thousands. The four had started their routine. They now had a public address system: a microphone and speaker had been borrowed from a local politician, Councillor Paddy Conway, so all of the 300 presnt could hear the hymns and prayers and respond. As usual the girls were standing together when above they could see the moon trying to break through the clouds. Her features became visible again and alongside was the headless blue statue. The lips were mimng the words 'Faith and Hope' and then continued, at pace with the hymns below, the words of 'Hail Queen of Heaven' and 'Be Not Afraid!'

Then to the left in the sky, they saw form in the clouds the Blessed Virgin, holding the infant Jesus. Below, in the darkness, fervour was spiced with awe and celebration. On this occasion several score confessed that they had shared in the visions.

The unusual continued on the following morning. A team of four County Council workers were sighted on the narrow road to Carns. They were surprised by the frequency of potholes in need of filling; three days of unprecedented traffic, increasing by the vision, had left fresh dents in the surface. Repairs were carried out and after hedges in the vicinity were neatly clipped, the workers went quietly off to more familiar terrain.

No carnival ever attracted such a tide of visitors to West Sligo. By the seventh night of the apparition the Gardai had worked out a well-tested method to help control the traffic. Many among the hordes were teenagers, a lot of them on bicycles, and some in hired buses. A retired gynacologist, with binoculars around his neck, was noticed by the local women. From Ballina eight miles away, a group of Saint John's Ambulance workers were now making the nightly journey.

This night was to produce the greatest confusion. It was between eleven o'clock and midnight when most of the three thousand present saw an orange ball shoot across the relatively bright sky. It passed over the crowds at great speed and then tailed off in the distance. Many saw what they made out to be three drops of blood coming from what they thought to be the Sacred Heart.

No more than a few minutes had passed before the next occurance. Several swore that the clouds above them opened and they became locked in a trace by light, whirring like a high-speed fan. Days later some told how their heads had nearly bursted at this time. Others saw the shape of the cross in the clouds. At the centre of the field, by the wooden post with the loudspeaker, the crowds were shoulder to shoulder. They were packed solid to the gate by the road, eighty yards away, and beyond it. Dozens were muted when they saw the Virgin Mary walking towards them from above before she disappeared. In her wake they sniffed what they took to be the smell of roses.

Among the visitors to Carns was Seamus Finn, editor of the *Sligo Chamion,* a local newspaper. He wrote: "Personally, I was sceptical before I arrived, I remained sceptical while I was there, and I am still sceptical. The only unusual thing I saw was ten thousand people standing in a field in prayerful vigil in the dark. . ."

I interviewed the four girls who claim to have seen the original apparition. You may believe them or not, but they refuse to be shaken from their claim. They all tell their story in a matter-of-fact manner, leaving it up to the listeners to make of it what they will. They do not seem in any way shattered or over-awed by their experience. On the contrary they seem composed and confident, despite the fact that they are now the centre of growing attention, with more and more people approaching them and asking to be touched. They take it all in their stride . . ."

As many as 10,000 came for the last night of the vigil. The necessity to keep a path free to ferry away the ill meant that all cars had to park along the main road, leaving a two mile walk for the crowds. Arrangements during daylight brought the formation of a local committee to help with stewarding. The volunteers wore blue ribands; on black boards was written 'No Smoking, No Flashing of Lights' or 'Apparition Site.'

The girs had decided they would gather here again on every feast day connected with the Blessed Virgin. (In fact they have prayed there each day since). A plan to collect money for a simple grotto is also in train.

In the early hours of the Wednesday night no signs of the supernatural had emerged. The crowds had been singing and praying. A nun was holding the lone microphone. "Please Mary," she asked, "come to me . . . I haven't seen your face. You showed yourself to others who have been her for nights but have not seen you. Please show yourself to me."

The plea dropped to a whisper that carried through the stillness.

"Mary, Mary, Mary, come to me . . ."

Later the girls were at the microphone once more. They recalled in a simple way how their lives had been changed. Four ordinary teenagers in rural Ireland who agreed that Bob Geldof is the person they most admire. Afterwards the crowds dispersed quietly into the night, without fuss.

A mouse couldn't trot across the road in West Sligo without Paul Conmy knowing of it. At 41 he has for 8 years represented the area on Sligo County Council and his political career is developing. He lives a mile from the field of the apparition and Mary Hanley, one of the four girls is his niece. He spent ten of the first 12 nights of vigils among the crowds at the site but saw nothing supernatural. He has watched on with interest.

"I believe that if I stood there at night, looking up at the sky for three or four hours, I would eventually see something. But at least two or three hundred people, a lot of them genuine people that I know, tell me they seen things like Our Lady and crosses. This place has changed. Fellas who would be outside the Church gaping in or chatting at the back are now inside praying and receiving. I know of a thirty year old who went to the vigil thinking that the people were getting soft. He saw something in the sky and he fell down on his face, and went hysterical. He had to be carried away. There's another fella and he went up there one night and whatever he saw, he started shakin' and he has it since. Another young lad who was up there slipped a disc when he fell into a drain and he is in hospital since. They started a collection for a grotto and I know that some English tourists gave £100. I saw a man giving twenty pounds: he said it was a small price to pay because the night before he had the privilege of seeing the Blessed Virgin. I've been talking to eighteen year olds and twenty year olds and instead of being away at discos or dances they are all up in the air about this thing.

"I brought the niece, Mary, back to the boarding school at Gortnor Abbey on the Wednesday, two days after she saw this apparition. She had packed her bags the next day and she was home again. The nun in the school came on the phone and she said now this girl had changed since before the holidays. She said she was completely different. Mary is a bit afraid since it happened; she won't sleep on her own; her mothers stays with her at night.

"Some nights now, if I'm driving alone by the field, I do bless myself. If I attend a funeral, and I can go to three or four some weeks, and I pass a statue of Our Lady I give a glance at it and the first thing that would hit you is, is it going to move? There's traffic out here all the time now. Some nights the cars are packed bumper to bumper. Imagine, a small local shop taking in £700 in three or four hours. I recognised a priest out here, one night, and he had a bright-coloured gabardine coat on, trying to disguise himself. Another night I saw a Reverend Mother: mustn't she believe there there is something?"

Councillor Conmy didn't take up the invitation to get involved in the local committee that works at vigils. Neither did he bring up the subject of the apparitions at County Council meetings. He feels it wouldn't be right to mix religion with politics.

Something is amiss at Carns.

Thousands of people are drawn to a remote field, in the dead of night. They walk silently along dark, narrow roads and in muck and rain, they pray. They are content. An atmosphere similar to that during the Pope's visit to Ireland prevails. A link with long ago when priests were on the run and a peasant people gathered at mass-rocks in subterfuge. The search is renewed for images and visions, dormant legacies drummed into minds and bones in convent schools and confessionals. Turmoil: a captive audience, head over heels with religious zeal, and a church that just doesn't know what to do about it.

Wexford Statues Move Away

Colm Tóibín

The new Dublin road from Enniscorthy by-passes the narrow, winding bridge at Scarawalsh. You can now make Ferns in about ten minutes. The church in Ferns is new as well, a fancy-looking, squat building made of glass and brick placed strategically at the crossroads. The church was broken into on a Friday night at the beginning of July. The tabernacle was robbed and consecrated hosts were thrown about the floor. Whoever broke in, and local people think they know who it was, also defecated on the floor of the church. It is also said that some of the hosts were taken out of the church to a party going on nearby where they were distributed, although there is no proof of this.

Camolin is just five minutes away on the Dublin side. For the past two weeks cars have lined both sides of the road from the village out to the shrine and a van selling hamburgers has been on duty. People believe that the moving statue has to do with the desecration of the church in Ferns; people believe that there is a direct connection.

Our companion in the back of the car was in Camolin the previous weekend; she did not see the statue moving. Instead, what she saw was a face appearing, a face on the statue looking towards a nearby house. It was the face of a young girl with fair hair cut in a fringe. Our companion was not standing in front of the statue when she saw this, but in her car some distance away waiting for her husband who was standing among the hundreds of people at the grotto. He stayed there for two hours and she was tired waiting for him. He did not realise that he had been away for so long and when she told him what she had seen he seemed somewhat irritated. As she started the car she saw him taking off his glasses and looking intently again at the statue. She asked him what he saw and he told her he saw a young girl's face on the statue, the face was looking up to the left, the girl's hair was fair

85

and cut in a fringe. He had seen exactly the same thing as she had seen.

This, a week later, was our third night at the shrine in Camolin and one thing was clear: the crowds were dying off. The hundreds who came the previous two weeks had dwindled to twenty or thirty. Cars no longer lined the main road. People, we were told, were more interested in going to Ballinspittle and were ready to travel all day and all night to do so.

The face of the statue at Camolin was lit by a torch. Nothing moved except the odd car speeding on the main road fifty yards away. There was an intense concentrated silence.

Someone started up the Rosary without any prompting. This had happened the other two nights as well. The people said the Rosary and stared at the statue, but no one seemed to see anything. Some people moved away and a few others came.

We went back to the car feeling that if the crowd had dwindled so drastically in just one week, then soon no one at all would go to the shrine in Camolin, it would be a two-week wonder. We sat for a while watching the small group pray and the statue above them when our companion said she saw it again. We looked clearly. We looked as hard as we could. She said she could see exactly what she had witnessed the previous weekend. But we could see nothing, except the dull face of the statue dimly lit by a torch. Our companion did not seem to experience any pleasure at what she saw, merely a sort of worried wonder. We sat there in silence. Suddenly a boy came and took the battery-run torch away so there was now no light on the face of the statue. We asked our companion if she could still see the face of a young girl on the statue and she said she couldn't, she said that with the torch gone she could see nothing. We stayed watching for a while longer.

There were two other moving statues in the area, we were told. One in Glenbrien on the road to Curracloe and the other outside Wexford town. On Friday night we drove down to Wexford arriving at around eleven o'clock. Just beyond the town on the main Rosslare road on the right hand side there is a rocky patch with some bushes growing. There is a statue of the Virgin standing against the rock. There is a turnstile which allows access to a number of seats and places to kneel.

There were about seventy people at the grotto. Again the Rosary was begun by someone at the front without any prompting. A bloke turned to me and asked me if I saw anything. I told him I didn't. He said he hadn't seen anything either but he had been to Ballinspittle and he had seen the statue move there. It had changed his life, he said. Four boys in their late teens stood up as close as they could to the statue and stared up at it. No one said they saw anything move. Over the next hour, as the pubs in Wexford closed, more people came out to look and the crowd swelled to a hundred but no more. Everyone seemed to be watching carefully, waiting anxiously for something to happen. As in Camolin, people came and went. It was after midnight when we left.

The following night we drove out to Glenbrien along an appalling, narrow, twisting road. There were crowds here all week we were told. We shoudn't miss this one. When we arrived we found one car in front of the lighted grotto and two men, just two men, standing looking at the images of Our Lady and Bernadette. They turned around to look at us. There was no one else around and there was a feeling that whatever excitement had occured at the grotto in Glenbrien was now over.

The statues had moved on.

*Inside the Church in Asdee
(photo Michael McSweeney)*

Seeing Is Believing

Fintan O'Toole

The revelations that week were disturbing. Sergeant Patrick Reilly told the Kerry Babies Tribunal in Tralee, twenty miles away, of how he had found the body of an infant on the rocks at White Strand. Mrs Mary Hayes said that if her daughter Kathleen had been calling out from the front door to Joanne in the field, the night Joanne had had the baby, she herself had heard nothing. A professor of oceanography was asked by James Duggan BL what would happen to an object the size of a newborn infant wrapped in a plastic bag and thrown into the sea off Slea Head. Worst was the evidence of Superintendent John Sullivan, outlining the course of the investigation into the death of the infant found at Cahirciveen, evidence which touched on dark things. They had, he said, checked into cases of incest, of married men known to have been associating with single girls, of a woman who was pregnant and went to England but might have returned. The parents of a girl whose diary contained references to rape were also interviewed. There were checks on itinerants and hippies. Somebody, he said, had even suggested that it might all be connected with black magic.

When the children of Asdee told their parents of what they had seen in the church, some of them thought of the terrible things that were being dragged to light in Tralee. "There was all that Kerry Babies business," says one father "and there have been other things too. There've been two murders in the Listowel area and over in Tarbert there was a case of a man who was having sex with his two nieces and got one of them pregnant. That's why some of the people here think that what's happened is a sign. There's a message there and it's to do with all the bad things that have been happening."

At twenty past twelve on the day that Superintendent Sullivan was giving evidence in Tralee, Thursday 14 February, Elizabeth

89

Flynn entered the little church of Saint Mary which is next door to her school in Asdee. Asdee is no more than a dip in the road from Ballybunion to Ballylongford, a tiny line of buildings of which the church, the school, two pubs and the shop-cum-petrol pump are the most notable. From down in the centre of the village's one street there is nothing to be seen but the straggling, sparsely populated dairying land around. From the brow of the hill where the village starts, however, the winking towers of industrial Ireland, the power stations of Moneypoint and Tarbert, loom up from the Shannon estuary. And in the estuary the long dark bulk of a 140,000 tonne coal carrier, the biggest ship ever to dock in an Irish port, lies at Moneypoint, clearly visible.

Elizabeth is seven and she goes to the church every day at lunchtime. She is making her first Communion this month. Mrs Eileen Moriarty, the principal teacher in the school is a devout, elderly woman and she encourages all her pupils to go next door to the church at lunchtime to "give two or three minutes to Jesus and the church." Elizabeth prayed to the two statues, painted plaster images of the Blessed Virgin and the Sacred Heart which stand in the alcove at the back of the church on the left hand side, separated by a brass trolley, surmounted with votive candles, and a small round stained glass porthole which lets in a dim diffuse light. Then she saw the Sacred Heart crook his finger and beckon her over to him. When she looked again, Our Lady's mouth was open.

Martin Fitzgerald, who is ten and is one of the altar boys in the church, was playing "hunting" out at the back of the school when Elizabeth Flynn and other "young ones" came up to him. They told him that the statues were moving. He went in with a large group of other children and looked at the statues for a while. He saw the head and eyes of one of the statues move. Some of the other children who were there at the same time saw nothing. Gradually all of the children gathered into the church to look. Altogether thirty-six of them now say that they saw the statues move in various ways. Some, like Blanaid Quane, have had more than one vision, seeing the statues move on different occasions up to the present. A few of their parents say that they too have seen movements in the statues.

In the Jesse James Tavern, next door to Saint Mary's church, the woman of the house keeps a small hard cover notebook behind the bar. The tavern has a low uneven ceiling, smoke stained walls and a sign on the wall facing the back door that says "Please use the toilet." Apart from the pool table, the juke box and the framed photographs of Jesse James that hang above the fireplace along with a Wanted Dead or Alive poster, it is an old style village pub. The juke box is on and the air is filled with the nasal tones of Tony Stevens singing a country and western song, Send Me No Roses, the B-side of the local anthem, The Village of Asdee. The notebook behind the bar is the legacy of the man who put Asdee on the map, the former parish priest Father Liam Ferris. It contains, in bold clear handwriting, a romantic version of the life and death of Jesse James, along with stories about his Asdee ancestors collected by Father Ferris from old people around the village.

Father Ferris dominated the village from the second world war until the end of the sixties, and he always believed that Asdee was marked out for a special distinction. A colourful and unorthodox man, he came to believe that the ancestors of Jesse James had come from Asdee and on 4 April every year he would say a solumn requiem mass, in the same church where the children would see the moving statues, for the repose of the soul of the greatest desperado of them all. He spent many years researching the connection about the James family. He touched the village with a sense of the extraordinary, and at the same time tried to encourage a simple piety, organising and encouraging devotion to Saint Eoin's holy well, half a mile from the village towards the estuary.

One of the stories in the notebook in the Jesse James Tavern concerns Saint Eoin's Well. In April 1965 Father Ferris wrote a story he had collected under the heading Blindness: "The James were Protestants. A servant girl of theirs was going blind and she went to the local holy well. She made a 'round' there and got her sight. At the same time her master had a horse gone blind. He took it to the holy well, and marched it around several times. The horse got its sight, but James, its owner, got blind."

Many people in Asdee still believe in the magical properties of Saint Eoin's well, particularly as a healer of diseases of the eyes. They say that some years ago a woman called Ellen Welch was praying there when she saw two fish in the water. She was immediately cured of her illness. They say that when the fish appear again in the water whoever sees them will be cured.

The last Saturday in April is one of the traditional days of worship at the well, a worship revived by Father Ferris. This year a few dozen people had gathered, walking up the winding tarmacadamed boreen and through the small rusting gate set among the hedges where a cardboard sign coloured with a child's hand says "The Holy Well". The well is a shallow pool of clear water fed by a sluggish spring. The thick bushes have been cleared from the water but encroach on three sides. On the fourth side some rough hewn stones serve as a kneeling place for the pilgrims to bend and scoop the blessed water up in a grey smoked glass coffee cup. In front of them at the far side of the pool is a small plaster virgin and child set on a blue and white square of tablecloth on the top of a rickety chair. The surrounding bushes are tied with clean white rags, pagan symbols of the flowering forth of May. The pilgrims mutter incessant rosaries. The following morning they will wait back after mass at ten and mutter the same rosaries before the statues at the back of Saint Mary's church.

Worship at the well had declined until the arrival of the present curate Father Michael O'Sullivan in Asdee a little over a year ago. He not only revived the worship at the well, but solemnised it, concelebrating Mass there late last summer with two other priests. There was a large turnout from the village and what one villager describes as a "tremendous atmosphere". There was singing in the still air of the holy place and a double rainbow encircled the well while the mass was in progress. Afterwards, a few of the villagers came to see this as a sign, a portent of what was to come.

The Holy Well and the notebook in the Jesse James Tavern are not Father Ferris' only legacies. He invested Asdee with a sense of other worlds. Father Ferris' views of the world were so unorthodox that in ecclesiastical circles the term "feresy" was coined to cover his many sub-heretical opinions.

He believed that all those who attended Mass should share in the sacred mysteries of the priesthood and thus that communion should be given in the hand. He believed that Moses, Plato and Aristotle should be canonised. He wrote a history of the world, The Story of Man, which featured the French Revolution only as a footnote on page 72. He invented a new world, called Pollantory, a place where souls went to have the good knocked out of them before they went to Hell, just as they went to

Purgatory to have the bad knocked out of them before they went to Heaven. And once, in one of the sermons in Saint Mary's church, which he would deliver with alternate sentences in English and Irish, he told the people of Asdee, in relation to Jesus walking on the water, that "anyone could walk on the water if they had enough ESB running through their bodies."

Father Ferris' many worlds mingled with the worlds of local folklore which was taught in the school by old Mr Moriarty, who died in 1981, a folklore which still holds a half belief among some of the village people. There are two hundred fairy forts in the vicinity of Asdee and some people claim to have seen lights going from one fort to another. There are stories of a drowned village under the sea between the nearby Beale Strand and Loop Head.

Father Michael O'Sullivan arrived as curate early in 1984. He had been a curate in Texas and had a strong belief in Padre Pio, the Italian monk who inspired great devotion because he appeared to carry the stigmata of Christ on his body. He himself had come through a serious operation and attributed his deliverance to the intercession of Padre Pio. His arrival sparked off a greater enthusiasm for the church and religion generally. He organised a party of villagers to clean up the small grotto, showing an apparition of the Blessed Virgin, which had fallen into a run-down state. He had Mass said at the Holy Well. And in November he started a Padre Pio prayer group, which would pray fervently every week against the encroaching evils of the world. A few weeks before the miracles of 14 February, Father O'Sullivan had a film about Padre Pio shown in the village and there was a good attendance, including many of the children.

The sacristan is filling the candle stalls at the back of the church with yet another box of votive candles. Forty little flames are flickering around the statues, causing shadowy movements on their painted surfaces. In the three months since the statues moved, the people of the village have come to take the miracles in their stride. "There have been so many miraculous movements in Asdee," says the sacristan "the people don't remark on them much anymore. The only thing we haven't had yet is a cure, and I'm sure that will come. But we've had a lot more movements than Knock has ever had."

There are now almost as many adults as children who claim to have seen movements in the statues — hands lifting, eyes moving, small spots appearing on the Blessed Virgin's neck. Some say they have smelt heavenly perfumes. "It's like a reminder that there is another world," says a woman across the street from the church. "And these things never happen except in poor little places like Asdee and Knock. Our Lady never appeared in Dublin."

Shortly after the movements were seen in Asdee, a group of children in Ballydesmond, a village on Kerry's border with Cork, saw the statues move in *their* local church. The people of Asdee are scornfully amused at the Ballydesmond stories. "Do you know what happened in Ballydesmond a few weeks ago?" asks one local man. "Two young fellas were in praying in the church one evening and the sacristan locked the door without checking if there was anyone inside. Well, a while later, weren't a few others walking down past the church and they heard these figures banging on the windows from the inside. Well they ran like the clappers over to the priest's house shouting 'Come quick father, the statues are trying to get out of the window'."

On the first Sunday after Asdee's apparitions, there were two thousand people in the village, a bigger crowd even than the one which had gathered the previous September when John Kennedy, who owns the shop and petrol pump in the village brought home the Sam Maguire Cup which he had helped to win as a member of the Kerry football team. Since then the stream of pilgrims has slowed, but it is still steady. And there have been more miracles. A man from Cavan who came on a Thursday evening to celebrate his wedding anniversary reached up to touch the statue of the Blessed Virgin, placing his fingertips on its hand. His finger and thumb, he claimed, were held firm in the statue's grasp for many seconds while he tried to release its hold. A woman who came in a busload from Newry one Sunday felt the Blessed Virgin take her hand in her own. The statue's hand, she said, turned to warm flesh as it gripped her. She was crying uncontrollably.

The miracles are noted down and placed through Father O'Sullivan's letterbox. Father O'Sullivan refers all queries to the diocesan office. Matters have been taken out of his hands. For the first few Sundays there were Stations of the Cross in the church and the rosary was relayed outside to the waiting crowds on a loudspeaker. The speaker still juts from the pebble-dashed church wall but it is now silent. Local people say that the order came from the bishop that the rosary was no longer to be relayed outside.

Many villagers still expect a message. Some thought there would be a message at Easter. When it didn't come, they simply carried on. "There will surely be a message," says a man whose daughter had two visions. "With all that's happening it wouldn't make sense if there was no message."

The pilgrims and petitioners who come are drawn not by miracles, but by the mundane miseries of the everyday world. From half past two on Sunday they bow their heads and step humbly into the twilight zone around the statues, the light from outside refracted from the rain and strained through the coloured glass. The older women cover their heads and mumble rosaries in unison. The younger women and most of the men stand stock still staring at the plaster images, their eyes not revealing whether they are daring or begging the statues to move. Red plump children play on the floor, their frustration held in check by occasional warnings.

Sometimes the petitioners scribble notes and leave them at the foot of either statue, mostly of the Blessed Virgin. A woman leaves a leaflet that proclaims the power of Holy Water — "the devil cannot long abide in a place or near a person that is often sprinkled with this blessed water." But mostly the petitions are more personal. "Our Blessed Lady, please bless all my family and help us sort out all our problems. Make Mam, Dad, better again and let us be one big family together forever." "Please help Gerard get a good job, I beg of you." "Please, please, help Jim to stop drinking and give us peace in our home." "Sacred Heart of Jesus, grant all my intentions and help me pay my bills." They fondle the hands of the statues continually, rubbing and stroking them. A woman takes a small white child's vest from her bag and rubs it to the statue of the Sacred Heart, then quickly replaces it and moves through the door. Now and then another candle gutters out and sends a last exhalation of smoke towards the roofbeams.

Magill, 16 May.

" This is it; and that is that. "